OPENING THE SEVENTH SEAL

OPENING THE SEVENTH SEAL

S. Ted Gashler

CFI
Springville, Utah

This is not an official publication of The Church of Jesus Christ of Latter-day Saints. The opinions and views expressed herein belong solely to the author and do not necessarily represent the opinions or views of Cedar Fort, Inc. Permission for the use of sources, graphics, and photos is also solely the responsibility of the author.

ISBN 13: 978-1-59955-265-1

Published by CFI, an imprint of Cedar Fort, Inc., 2373 W. 700 S., Springville, UT 84663
Distributed by Cedar Fort, Inc. www.cedarfort.com

LIBRARY OF CONGRESS CATALOGING-IN-PUBLICATION DATA
Gashler, S. Ted (Sheridan Ted), 1939-
Opening the seventh seal / S. Ted Gashler.
p. cm.
ISBN 978-1-59955-265-1
1. End of the world. 2. Church of Jesus Christ of Latter-day Saints--Doctrines. 3. Mormon Church--Doctrines. 4. Apocalyptic literature--Mormon authors. I. Title.

BX8643.E83G37 2009
236'.9--dc22

2009002998

Cover design by Angela D. Olsen
Cover design © 2009 by Lyle Mortimer
Edited and typeset by Melissa J. Caldwell

Printed in the United States of America

10 9 8 7 6 5 4 3 2 1

Printed on acid-free paper

Trust in the Lord with all thine heart; and lean not unto thine own understanding. In all thy ways acknowledge him, and he shall direct thy paths.
Proverbs 3:5–6

CONTENTS

Introduction

Life is never what we expect it to be. That Ted Gashler is even writing an LDS book is itself a strange twist of fate. Had his mother not died when he was a child, he would most likely never have even heard about the LDS Church. However, because his dad owned a creamery and bought milk from an LDS farmer whose daughter was willing to raise three stepchildren, The Church of Jesus Christ of Latter-day Saints has affected every aspect of Ted's life from that moment on—a legacy that has ultimately enabled him to touch the lives of thousands of people.

After receiving a BS in Agricultural Education at Utah State University, Ted received an MBA in Agribusiness Administration from Clayton University, and an honorary PhD in International Agribusiness Administration from Bila Tzerkva Agricultural University in Ukraine. He taught agribusiness and dairy science at Oregon State University, and then went on to Northcentral Technical College in Wausau, Wisconsin, where he served as associate Dean of Agriculture. While at NTC, he had the opportunity to write numerous grants bringing over a hundred students from the former Soviet Union to study agriculture in the United States. After eight years at NTC, he became a Country Director of a USAID funded organization, which led him to a year in Macedonia and two years in Ukraine, where he directed numerous agricultural and agribusiness projects. These projects included everything from establishing the first privately owned meat processing plant in Ukraine, to creating an electrical generating plant in Macedonia, powered by methane gas that came from the manure of a very large hog farm. By 1996, every agricultural university and institute in the Ukraine ran Farm Business and Production Management programs modeled after the program he supervised in Wisconsin.

In 1998, Ted was called to be the mission president of the Russia Samara Mission, a mission that covered a large land mass that included three time zones, and which gave him the opportunity to observe agriculture over a very large area. There he realized he had to write this book:

> As we drove from one part of the mission to another, I couldn't help but think about the prophesied famines and destruction that will happen. During this time I often pondered on the importance of getting our members ready for these calamities and helping as many as possible of God's other children to see the light also. I knew I had to write it because my background in agriculture and international affairs along with an understanding of the signs of the times made me one of the few people qualified to realize that a world famine is imminent. This is a book of warning—in words that are clear and to the point. I say what needs to be said *now.* Time is of the essence.

Why This Book Was Written

Twice in my life I have suddenly and unexpectedly felt a compelling urge that I must do something that I had never done before or even thought of doing. Both times it seemed the task was above and beyond my capabilities, but I was encouraged, inspired, and driven until the job was accomplished. In areas where I was weak, the Lord was always there, leading me to those who could and would help me accomplish the goal as I was inspired.

The first time this happened was in 1984 when Elder Jacob de Jager came to Wisconsin to speak at our district conference. His twenty-minute talk in the priesthood session completely changed the course of my future and my family's. Elder de Jager admonished us to get ready for "the world is about to change." He said all the nations of the earth were being prepared by the Lord to hear the gospel, and it would be a short time until many countries would be opened up to the gospel. This meeting also greatly changed the life of one of my sons, who was sixteen years old at that time. On the way home he said, "Dad, I need to get out of my band class and take Mandarin Chinese." The next day he dropped out of band and took a BYU correspondence class in Mandarin Chinese. Upon graduation from high school, he went to the Air Force Academy. Two years later he was called on a mission to Taiwan. After his mission he completed his studies at the Air Force Academy and became a pilot flying F-16s. Later he was assigned to train the Taiwan Air Force how to fly F-16s. He is now a commercial airline pilot and serves as an Air Attache to Beijing China.

Elder de Jagers' talk inspired me in a different way. I was directed to write a grant that would provide funds to bring students from Poland and Hungry to the United States for training in agribusiness at Northcentral Technical College in Wisconsin where I was associate dean of agriculture at that time. I wrote the grant with no luck and then rewrote it each year for several years, and finally in 1988 we were successful in obtaining the funds necessary to bring forty-five students from Poland and Hungary to our college for training in agribusiness.

I then had the opportunity to go to these countries to select the students that would be in the program. While in each country, I was able to study the infrastructure of agriculture, agribusiness, and government as well as the people of these nations. Working in these countries and getting to know and understand the people was the beginning of the complete change of direction my life would take.

During the summers of 1990 through 1993, I served as a volunteer on numerous agribusiness assignments in the countries of Poland, Kazakhstan, Russia, Bulgaria, Macedonia, and Hungary for Volunteers in Overseas Cooperative Assistance (VOCA), a private non-profit organization funded by the United States Agency for International Development (USAID). VOCA provides technical assistance to cooperatives, other private agribusinesses, and related government agencies abroad. U.S. volunteer specialists accomplish this work through short-term technical assistance. VOCA works only at the request of host-country organizations. In each of these countries, I was able to work with government leaders and others involved at every level of agriculture and agribusiness. This was the best possible opportunity for me to learn about both agriculture and government infrastructure during the communist era and the changes that were taking place in the early nineties.

In 1993, I was offered a full time job with VOCA as representative in Macedonia. I took that position, and between June of 1993 and June 1994, we completed 164 agribusiness projects in Macedonia. Then, in 1994, I was transferred to Ukraine where I worked until September 1996. These experiences gave me a broad understanding of agriculture and government in the countries of the former Soviet Union.

Then, in 1998, I was called to preside over the Russia Samara Mission for The Church of Jesus Christ of Latter-day Saints.

Because of these unique opportunities I had to live and work in such diverse places during this twelve-year period, and I could not help but see the massive disintegration of the agricultural infrastructure that had been present and somewhat successful under seventy years of communism. I saw the social devastations resulting from human misery, negligence, apathy, and greed. As I observed this desolation, I found myself returning again and again to the scriptures and especially to the Book of Revelation to try to understand the predicted famines and upcoming plagues and other signs of the times that will be poured out upon the earth.

It was at this time that I once again felt a need to do something I had never done before, which was to write this book, so it could help others to understand what I had learned firsthand by living in many parts of the world where the "signs of the times" have begun. I started looking at what was happening in the former Soviet Union, and then studied the rest of the world while I was living and working in northwestern China.

I began by researching HIV (AIDS) in Russia and discovered that in 2000, there were only eleven documented cases of AIDS in the city of Togliatti, Russia. Just one year later, Russian government affirmed that Togliatti had over three thousand officially reported cases of HIV. Health officials predicted that the actual number of cases might be ten times that number. In the city of St. Petersburg, public health authorities are finding that, as many as one quarter of the youth they screen at free clinics are positive for HIV. Russian health authorities are concerned that the number of HIV-infected Russians will soon reach one million.[1]

Documented cases of HIV infection rates among intravenous drug abusers throughout Russia continues to rise at an alarming rate, increasing from a small percentage in 1997 to over 50 percent in 2000. HIV infections continue to multiply due to: (1) substantial increases in intravenous drug abuse in Russian youth, (2) growing prostitution and promiscuity, and (3) limited public health awareness. It was disheartening to discover that the population of the Russian Federation declined by 768,000 or 0.5 percent in 2000, due mainly to high mortality from tobacco and alcohol-related illnesses, and continued declines in the birthrate.[2]

What is the future outlook for Russia? The average male life expectancy in Russia is now only fifty-seven years and is unlikely to improve anytime soon. Tobacco and alcohol use among men remains at epidemic proportions. HIV is rapidly becoming one of the leading killers of Russian youth. Heavy drinking, poor nutrition and medical care, and environmental pollution plague Russia.

And, unfortunately, so it goes all over the world to one extent or another. But these are only the beginning of the plagues the planet now faces. This is why this book needed to be written. I hope this book will help prepare those who will listen to put their life in order and get ready. It has begun.

Notes

1. Russian Public Health Review, January 2002

2. Brian Mac Intyre, "Russia Population Shrinks," *Salt Lake Tribune,* Oct. 23, 2001.

1

Opening the Seventh Seal

The plagues of the last days have started. This has become increasingly apparent since the terrible disaster of September 11, 2001. Government leaders, terrorists, and gangs are ripening in iniquity and becoming expert in creating new and improved ways to kill. Pride, vanity, and evil of all kinds have overcome the hearts and minds of many people of the world—and many leaders as well. Now vexation is the reward we are beginning to reap: "When the righteous are in authority, the people rejoice: but when the wicked beareth rule, the people mourn" (Proverbs 29:2).

In this day, men have become wise in their own eyes, no longer fearing the Lord. Instead, many devise mischief continually while running to evil. (See Proverbs 1:16; Isaiah 59:7; Acts 13:10; 3 Nephi 16:10). Many of this planet's population now proudly exhibit all the abominations the Lord hates: "A proud look, a lying tongue, and hands that shed innocent blood, An heart that deviseth wicked imaginations, feet that be swift in running to mischief, A false witness that speaketh lies, and he that soweth discord among brethren" (Proverbs 6:17–19).

Today we are just beginning to see the fruits of what happens when men follow the gods of their own making and seek the praise of man rather than following the counsel and commandments of the Lord. Many have forgotten what the duty of man is. "Let us hear the conclusion of the whole matter: Fear God, and keep his commandments: for this is the *whole* duty of man" (Ecclesiastes 12:13; emphasis added).

The scriptures contain much information about the era we are now beginning. The ancient prophets were shown our day, and they described it throughout the scriptures. The prophet who went into the greatest detail about this time period was John the Revelator. The book of Revelation, though somewhat cryptic, provides the most details about our times. Fortunately, Revelation is made easier to understand by the Prophet Joseph Smith. His teachings and commentary in the Doctrine and Covenants concerning the Revelation of John help us understand the things John knew that we would need to know in this day and age. Doctrine and Covenants section 77 provides clarity on many of the questions that are not answered in the Bible alone.

With the aid of Doctrine and Covenants 77, we see that the first four chapters are a history of the world from its beginning up to John's era. Chapter 5 is a prelude for the remaining chapters of Revelation that center on the seven seals. Chapters 6 through 22 concentrate on the seven seals.

Opening of the Seven Seals

The book of Revelation is a review of what has happened on the earth since the Fall of Adam, and what we can expect from this time until the Second Coming of Jesus Christ.

Each of the seven seals represents a thousand years since the Fall of Adam. The time period from now until the Second Coming of Jesus Christ is described in the greatest detail of any of the seals. Doctrine and Covenants states:

> We are to understand that it [speaking of chapter six of the Book of Revelations] contains the revealed will, mysteries, and the works of God; the hidden things of his economy concerning this earth during the seven thousand years of its continuance, or its temporal existence.
>
> We are to understand that the first seal contains the things of the first thousand years, and the second also of the second thousand years, and so on until the seventh. (D&C 77:6–7)

Will he come ten or fifty or a hundred years after the opening of the seventh seal? Or will his various appearances be interspersed with the signs of the times that are reserved for that future day? Answers to these and similar questions have been withheld from us and will be known only as the various events transpire. However, Elder Bruce R. McConkie wrote in 1982,

> We are now living in the Saturday night of time; the millennial

> morning will soon dawn. This is the end of the sixth seal, and the seventh seal will soon be opened. Our modern revelation tells us plainly that Christ will come sometime after the opening of seventh seal; it will be during the seventh thousand years and after the events listed in the eighth chapter of John's writings. The plagues and woes there recited shall all take place during the seventh seal, and they are "the preparing of the way before the time of his coming" (D&C 77:12).[1]

Note that Revelation 5 explains that only Christ can open the book and loose the seven seals. No one else was given the authority to accomplish this task.

Only God the Father knows when the Second Coming of Jesus Christ will occur: "But of that day and hour knoweth no man, no, not the angels of heaven, but my Father only" (Matthew 24:36). Revelation does, however, provide the general time frame and shows the events that will lead up to the Second Coming. Revelation 6:1–2 describes the opening of the first seal. This represents the first thousand years since the Fall of Adam. In The Church of Jesus Christ of Latter-day Saints' King James edition of the Bible, we find that the Fall of Adam occurred in 4000 B.C. (see the chronological tables in the Bible Dictionary, page 635).

Revelation 6:3–4 details the opening of the second seal, that is, the events that occurred in the second thousand years since the Fall of Adam. At this date, most of the events that were to happen through the first six seals have happened.

The following is a table of the approximate thousand year time periods for the opening of each seal:

1. Opening of the first seal—about 4000 B.C. to 3000 B.C. (Revelation 6:1–2).
2. Opening of the second seal—about 3000 B.C. to 2000 B.C. (Revelation 6:3–4).
3. Opening of the third seal—about 2000 B.C. to 1000 B.C. (Revelation 6:5–6).
4. Opening of the fourth seal—about 1000 B.C. to A.D. 1 (Revelation 6:7–8).
5. Opening of the fifth seal—about A.D. 1 to A.D. 1000 (Revelation 6:9–11).
6. Opening of the sixth seal—about A.D. 1000 to A.D. 2000 (Revelation 6:12–7:17).

7. Opening of the seventh seal—about A.D. 2000 to A.D. 3000 (Revelation 8–22).

We see in Revelation 8:1 that the seventh seal was to be opened in approximately A.D. 2000. If, in fact, 2000 is the year, then we are now living in the time period of the seventh seal. I believe that the seventh seal most likely has been opened, and we are probably now living in the era of the seventh seal.

Silence for the Space of Half an Hour

Revelation 8:1 is a key verse to our understanding of what will transpire from now until Christ returns to reign as King of Kings. Chapters 8–22 describe the desolation that will be poured out during the seventh seal preceding the Second Coming. "And when he had opened the seventh seal, there was silence in heaven about the space of half an hour" (Revelation 8:1). To understand this verse and the wars and plagues that will be poured out during the seventh seal discussed in chapters 8 and 9, the period before the Lord comes, we must first turn to Doctrine and Covenants 77:12–13:

> 12. "Q. What are we to understand by the sounding of the trumpets, mentioned in the 8th chapter of Revelation?
>
> A. We are to understand that as God made the world in six days, and on the seventh day he finished his work, and sanctified it, and also formed man out of the dust of the earth, even so, in the beginning of the seventh thousand years will the Lord God sanctify the earth, and complete the salvation of man, and judge all things, and shall redeem all things . . . unto the end of all things; and the sounding of the trumpets of the seven angels are the preparing and finishing of his work, in the beginning of the seventh thousand years—the preparing of the way before the time of his coming.
>
> 13. Q. When are the things to be accomplished, which are written in the 9th chapter of Revelation?
>
> A. They are to be accomplished after the opening of the seventh seal, before the coming of Christ" (D&C 77:12–13).

D&C 88:95–96 echoes Revelation 8:1 and offers further insight into this period of silence:

> And there shall be silence in heaven for the space of half an hour; and immediately after shall the curtain of heaven be unfolded, as a

> scroll is unfolded after it is rolled up, and the face of the Lord shall be unveiled; and the saints that are upon the earth, who are alive, shall be quickened and be caught up to meet him" (D&C 88:95–96).

It is important to understand that the half an hour spoken of is not a half an hour in man's time, but a half an hour in the Lord's time. 2 Peter explains the Lord's time: "But, beloved, be not ignorant of this one thing, that one day is with the Lord as a thousand years, and a thousand years as one day" (2 Peter 3:8).

The Book of Abraham similarly observes that one day of the Lord is a thousand years in our time:

> And the Lord said unto me, by the Urim and Thummim, that Kolob was after the manner of the Lord, according to its times and seasons in the revolutions thereof; that one revolution was a day unto the Lord, after his manner of reckoning, it being one thousand years according unto the time appointed to that whereon thou standest. This is the reckoning of the Lord's time, according to the reckoning of Kolob. (Abraham 3:4)

When we fully comprehend that a thousand years in our time is but a day in the Lord's time, then we can grasp the importance of Revelation 8:1. "And when he had opened the seventh seal, there was silence in heaven about the space of half an hour" (Revelation 8:1). If a thousand years is one day in the Lord's time, then a half an hour would be 1000 years divided by 24 hours in a day, which equals 41.667 years is an hour of the Lord's time. So one half hour would be 41.667 divided by 2 equals 20.83333 years, or roughly 21 years.

Has the silence from heaven begun? We cannot jump to any conclusions as to when these events will actually transpire—we must always remember that only God the Father knows all things, including when the Second Coming of Jesus Christ will occur. "For the time is at hand; the day or the hour no man knoweth; but it surely shall come" (D&C 39:21). Yet one thing is certain. Time is running out. If we are prudent, we will get our lives and our houses in order, listen to, and observe the counsel of our prophets, and stand in holy places. This reasoning becomes even more significant when we consider the revelation, which states categorically that Christ will come in the beginning of the seventh thousand years of its temporal existence (D&C 77:6, 12).

What is the desolation to be poured out with the opening of the seventh seal? Matthew 24 provides a good overview of the wars and rumors of wars, famines, pestilences, earthquakes, false prophets, false Christs, and so on. Revelation 8 and 9 give us a grim but accurate view of what we can expect—starting with voices—the voices of thunderings and lightnings, and earthquakes (Revelation 8:5)—and moving right along to hail and fire mingled with blood, where one-third of the trees and grass will burn (Revelation 8:7), followed by a great mountain burning with fire to be cast into the sea and one-third of the sea becoming blood (Revelation 8:8). And so on through all the plagues and desolation that will be poured out during this time frame.

Joseph Fielding Smith wrote: "This is, and will be, in the nature of the cleansing process to prepare the earth and its inhabitants, those who will be fortunate enough to remain for the coming of our Savior when he shall commence his reign for a thousand years upon the earth. The knowledge that the time of its fulfillment is at hand should cause all men some thoughtful sober thinking."[2]

I truly believe these things will all happen just as stated in the scriptures. Therefore, the rest of this book will addressed the plagues, famine, and all desolation leading up to the fall of Babylon and the dragon. I will also discuss what we the members of the Church can do to get ready for this time and what we can do to help prepare God's other children for the Second Coming of Jesus Christ.

Notes

1. Bruce R. McConkie, *The Millennial Messiah: The Second Coming of the Son of Man* (Salt Lake City: Deseret Book, 1982), 382.

2. Joseph Fielding Smith, *Church History and Modern Revelation,* 4 vols. (Salt Lake City: The Church of Jesus Christ of Latter-day Saints, 1946–1949), 2: 72.

2

UNDERSTANDING THE PLAGUES OF THE LAST DAYS

This is one of the most exciting times to be living on the earth. We will have an opportunity to witness and even be a part of many of the great and dreadful events of the last days. The events of the last days that have been prophesied about since the beginning of time are now beginning to occur. The wars and rumors of wars, pestilence, plagues, famines, and unbelievable suffering and misery have started and will only get worse. But those of us who choose to be on the Lord's side and serve him and do our part in spreading the gospel will bring eternal happiness to people who would otherwise know only eternal pain and suffering. I am excited. We are spreading the good news, while much of the world will be filled with the abomination of desolation.

> And I saw another sign in heaven, great and marvellous, seven angels having the seven last plagues; for in them is filled up the wrath of God. (Revelation 15:1)

> And plagues shall go forth, and they shall not be taken from the earth until I have completed my work, which shall be cut short in righteousness. (D&C 84:97)

> For a desolating scourge shall go forth among the inhabitants of the earth, and shall continue to be poured out from time to time, if they repent not, until the earth is empty, and the inhabitants thereof are consumed away and utterly destroyed by the brightness of my coming. (D&C 5:19)

> And there shall be men standing in that generation, that shall not

pass until they shall see an overflowing scourge; for a desolating sickness shall cover the land. But my disciples shall stand in holy places, and shall not be moved; but among the wicked, men shall lift up their voices and curse God and die. (D&C 45:31–32)

The above scriptures leave us with no doubt that terrible plagues will cover the earth in the last days. They will make the Black Death seem like child's play in comparison. These judgments will be poured out on the nations of the earth because of the rejection of the gospel:

> And thus, with the sword and by bloodshed the inhabitants of the earth shall mourn; and with famine, and plague, and earthquake, and the thunder of heaven, and the fierce and vivid lightning also, shall the inhabitants of the earth be made to feel the wrath, and indignation, and chastening hand of an Almighty God, until the consumption decreed hath made a full end of all nations. (D&C 87:6)

If one is to understand the plagues of the last days, it is necessary to have at least a basic knowledge of the sixteenth chapter of Revelation. Because of its importance, I will attempt to describe this chapter in ways that will help everyone to understand. The significant concepts of each verse will be highlighted and then an explanation will follow.

In the fifteenth and sixteenth chapters of Revelation, John was shown the last seven plagues. From this, we see that God in his mercy will pour out terrible and devastating plagues on the wicked and ungodly in the last days. These plagues and diseases will destroy a large percentage of the people of this earth in preparation for the final cleansing, which will prepare the world as a place for the righteous to live, and where Christ will reign as Lord of Lords and King of Kings. (See Revelation 15–16).

The First Angel

In Revelation 16, verse 2, we learn that the first plague will be "a noisome and grievous sore:"

> And the first went, and poured out his vial upon the earth; and there fell a noisome and grievous sore upon the men which had the mark of the beast, and upon them which worshipped his image.

This could well be the plague discussed by Zechariah:

> And this shall be the plague wherewith the Lord will smite all the people that have fought against Jerusalem; Their flesh shall consume

> away while they stand upon their feet, and their eyes shall consume away in their holes, and their tongue shall consume away in their mouth. (Zechariah 14:12)

This also sounds like what is described in the Doctrine and Covenants 29.

> Wherefore, I the Lord God will send forth flies upon the face of the earth, which shall take hold of the inhabitants thereof, and shall eat their flesh, and shall cause maggots to come in upon them; And their tongues shall be stayed that they shall not utter against me; and their flesh shall fall from off their bones, and their eyes from their sockets. (D&C 29:18–19)

These noisome and grievous sores and other terrible plagues could well be the results of what man brings on himself through chemical, biological, or nuclear warfare.

The Second Angel

The second plague poured out by the second angel discussed in Revelation is the turning the waters of the sea to blood. "And the second angel poured out his vial upon the sea; and it became as the blood of a dead man: and every living soul died in the sea" (Revelation 16:3).

This plague is more fully described in Revelation 8:8–9:

> And the second angel sounded, and as it were a great mountain burning with fire was cast into the sea: and the third part of the sea became blood; And the third part of the creatures which were in the sea, and had life, died; and the third part of the ships were destroyed.

This sounds like the plague the Lord was talking about in modern scripture:

> Behold, I, the Lord, in the beginning blessed the waters; but in the last days, by the mouth of my servant John, I cursed the waters. Wherefore, the days will come that no flesh shall be safe upon the waters. (D&C 61:14–15).

Again this could be the fallout of chemical, biological, and nuclear warfare. It also could be in part the great pollutions caused by man in the last days from sewage dumped into the water, runoff from industrial chemicals, highways, farms, feedlots, chemical treatment plants, and similar things.

The Third Angel

The third plague will be when the third angel turns the rivers and fountains to blood. At this time, all drinking water will become polluted and diseased. "And the third angel poured out his vial upon the rivers and fountains of water; and they became blood" (Revelation 16:4).

We know that the Lord can do all things and we know he has turned the waters to blood in the past when it was necessary. And we know he will do it again.

> Thus saith the Lord, In this thou shalt know that I am the Lord: behold, I will smite with the rod that is in mine hand upon the waters which are in the river, and they shall be turned to blood. And the fish that is in the river shall die, and the river shall stink; and the Egyptians shall lothe to drink of the water of the river. (Exodus 7:17–18)

We also know that the Lord will give two of his prophets the power to shut heaven, so it won't rain and they will also be able turn the waters to blood:

> These have power to shut heaven, that it rain not in the days of their prophecy: and have power over waters to turn them to blood, and to smite the earth with all plagues, as often as they will. (Revelation 11:6)

> Behold, I, the Lord, in the beginning blessed the waters; but in the last days, by the mouth of my servant John, I cursed the waters. Wherefore, the days will come that no flesh shall be safe upon the waters. (D&C 61:14–15)

Presently though, I think man is trying to do the job for the third angel. Man is polluting the rivers, lakes, underground aquifer and the oceans at alarming rates. Water pollution is now a major worldwide problem that is happening because of man's disregard for the environment—and because of greed.

Numerous studies have reported that more than a billion people now lack safe, clean, and reliable water, and the problem will continue to worsen. The problem will soon affect more than forty countries. Experts report that water-related diseases presently kill from five to seven million people annually, and up to half of the population of the developing world suffers from water pollution diseases at any given time. Pollution affects water supplies even when there is no shortage of water. The fouling of the waterways and surrounding river basins have contributed to millions of environmental refuges in the last few years.

I believe one of the largest threats to the water supply will be the pollution from chemical, biological, and nuclear fallout when the wars and rumors of wars heat up around the planet:

> And the third angel sounded, and there fell a great star from heaven, burning as it were a lamp, and it fell upon the third part of the rivers, and upon the fountains of waters; And the name of the star is called wormwood: and the third part of the waters became wormwood; and many men died of the waters, because they were made bitter. (Revelation 8:10–11)

An interesting fact is that this has happened to some extent already. The fallout from the Chernobyl catastrophe caused exactly this kind of damage to the rivers, lakes, and soil.

This single incident killed thousands of people and polluted the environment for generations to come. (An interesting note is that Chernobyl means *wormwood* in Russian.)

Verses 5–7 show that all the angels in heaven agree that the Lord is just in his dealing with the wicked.

The Fourth Angel

The fourth angel's plague will be to change the effects of the sun so men will be scorched with fire and extreme heat:

> And the fourth angel poured out his vial upon the sun; and power was given unto him to scorch men with fire. And men were scorched with great heat, and blasphemed the name of God, which hath power over these plagues: and they repented not to give him glory. (Revelation 16: 8–9)

Again, it appears that mankind is helping the fourth angel to accomplish his task of global warming. The earth's climate is already changing because human activities are altering the chemical composition of the atmosphere through the buildup of greenhouse gases—primarily carbon dioxide, methane, and nitrous oxide. The heat-trapping property of these gases is undisputed.

The greenhouse gas concentrations are increasing because of the combustion of fossil fuels and other human activities. The primary reason is the increased concentration of carbon dioxide. Fossil fuels burned to run motor vehicles, heat homes and businesses, and power factories are responsible for about 98 percent of the carbon dioxide emissions, 24 percent of methane emissions, and 18 percent of nitrous oxide emissions. Increased agriculture, deforestation, landfills, industrial production, and mining also contribute a significant share of emissions. In 1997 the United States emitted about one-fifth of the total global greenhouse gases. Global mean surface temperatures have increased 0.5–1.0 F since the late nineteenth century. The twentieth century's ten warmest years all occurred in the last fifteen years of the century. Of these, 1998 was the warmest year on record. The snow cover in the northern hemisphere and the floating ice in the Arctic Ocean has decreased. Globally, sea level has risen 4 to 8 inches over the past century. Increased concentrations of greenhouse gases are likely to accelerate the rate of climate change.[1]

Yet the global warming will only be the beginning and a part of it, as the Lord has assured us:

> Wherefore, all those who are proud, and that do wickedly, the day that cometh shall burn them up, saith the Lord of Hosts, for they shall be as stubble. And they shall be visited with thunderings, and lightnings, and earthquakes, and all manner of destructions, for the fire of the anger of the Lord shall be kindled against them, and they shall be as stubble, and the day that cometh shall consume them, saith the Lord of Hosts. (2 Nephi 26:4, 6)

> For after today cometh the burning—this is speaking after the manner of the Lord—for verily I say, tomorrow all the proud and they that do wickedly shall be as stubble; and I will burn them up, for I am the Lord of Hosts; and I will not spare any that remain in Babylon. (D&C 64:24)

We know the reason the wicked will be burned is because they will not repent and turn to God. But instead they become grosser in their evil ways:

> And the rest of the men which were not killed by these plagues yet repented not of the works of their hands, that they should not worship devils, and idols of gold, and silver, and brass, and stone, and of wood: which neither can see, nor hear, nor walk: Neither repented they of their murders, nor of their sorceries, nor of their fornication, nor of their thefts. (Revelation 9:20–21)

The good news for the righteous is that the sunlight and the heat will not affect them:

> They shall hunger no more, neither thirst any more; neither shall the sun light on them, nor any heat. For the Lamb which is in the midst of the throne shall feed them, and shall lead them unto living fountains of waters: and God shall wipe away all tears from their eyes. (Revelation 7:16–17)

The Fifth Angel

The fifth plague will be the spread of spiritual darkness, pain, and misery to those who do not follow the Lord:

> And the fifth angel poured out his vial upon the seat of the beast; and his kingdom was full of darkness; and they gnawed their tongues for pain, And blasphemed the God of heaven because of their pains and their sores, and repented not of their deeds. (Revelation 16:10–11)

Darkness covers the kingdom of the devil. I believe this darkness is both physical and spiritual:

> For, behold, the darkness shall cover the earth, and gross darkness the people: but the Lord shall arise upon thee; and his glory shall be seen upon thee. (Isaiah 60:2)

We are warned to watch out for this darkness as the devil is spreading it everywhere throughout the world.

> Therefore, what I say unto one I say unto all: Watch, for the adversary spreadeth his dominions, and darkness reigneth. (D&C 82:5)

Does this sound like the darkness and misery that man is bringing on himself by disregarding the commandments of the Lord? What about AIDS—isn't this an example of spiritual darkness in the last days?

President Ezra Taft Benson speaking at BYU in 1987, said the following about AIDS:

> The world is already beginning to reap the consequences of their abandonment of any standards of morality. As just one example, the Secretary of the Department of Health and Human Services in the United States, warned that if a cure for AIDS is not quickly found, it could become a worldwide epidemic that "will dwarf such earlier medical disasters as the black plague, smallpox, and typhoid. (Salt Lake

> Tribune, 30 January 1987, p. A-1). As the world seeks solution for this disease, which began primarily through widespread homosexuality, they look everywhere but to the law of the Lord. There are numerous agencies, both public and private, trying to combat AIDS. They seek increased funding for research. They sponsor programs of education and information. They write bills aimed at protecting the innocent from infection. They set up treatment programs for those who have already become infected. These are important and necessary programs and we commend those efforts. But why is it we rarely hear anyone calling for a return to chastity, for a commitment to virtue and fidelity?[2]

In verse 10 the Lord showed John a kingdom that was full of darkness where they gnawed their tongues for pain. Those who choose spiritual darkness rather than living the commandments of the Lord may look forward to that kind of pain.

> The Lord will smite thee with the botch of Egypt, and with the emerods, and with the scab, and with the itch, whereof thou canst not be healed.
>
> The Lord shall smite thee with madness, and blindness, and astonishment of heart:
>
> And thou shalt grope at noonday, as the blind gropeth in darkness, and thou shalt not prosper in thy ways: and thou shall be only oppressed and spoiled evermore, and no man shall save thee. (Deuteronomy 28:27–29)

The Lord has warned us that now is the time for each of us to get completely out of Babylon. He has told us that now would be a good time for each of us to give ourselves what I like to call a "check-up from the neck up"—meaning to make sure we are entirely on the Lord's side.

> Verily, verily, I say unto you darkness covereth the earth, and gross darkness the minds of the people, and all flesh has become corrupt before my face. (D&C 112:23)

And further,

> And the whole world lieth in sin, and groaneth under darkness and under the bondage of sin.
>
> And by this you may know they are under the bondage of sin, because they come not unto me.
>
> For whoso cometh not unto me is under the bondage of sin.

> And whoso receiveth not my voice is not acquainted with my voice, and is not of me.
>
> And your minds in times past have been darkened because of unbelief, and because you have treated lightly the things you have received—
>
> Which vanity and unbelief have brought the whole church under condemnation.
>
> And this condemnation resteth upon the children of Zion, even all.
>
> And they shall remain under this condemnation until they repent and remember the new covenant, even the Book of Mormon and the former commandments which I have given them, not only to say, but to do according to that which I have written—
>
> That they may bring forth fruit meet for their Father's kingdom; otherwise there remaineth a scourge and judgment to be poured out upon the children of Zion.
>
> For shall the children of the kingdom pollute my holy land? Verily, I say unto you, Nay (D&C 84:49–59)

When the fifth angel pours out his vial on the earth, spiritual darkness will abound. The great and abominable church, the whore of all the earth, will be consumed with darkness. For the gain of filthy lucre and the praise of man, it will teach the doctrines of man and Satan. Light and truth will diminish as evil and darkness increase until Babylon falls. During this time period the world will become the most wicked it has ever been in the entire history of the planet. Evil will continue to grow until this terrible plague of spiritual darkness causes the end of the world as we know it.

And again the plague of spiritual darkness may also include the effects of chemical, biological and nuclear war that man will bring upon himself.

The Sixth Angel

The sixth plague will be the drying up of Euphrates River:

> And the sixth angel poured out his vial upon the great river Euphrates; and the water thereof was dried up, that the way of the kings of the east might be prepared.
>
> And I saw three unclean spirits like frogs come out of the mouth of the dragon, and out of the mouth of the beast, and out of the mouth of the false prophet.

> For they are the spirits of devils, working miracles, which go forth unto the kings of the earth and of the whole world, to gather them to the battle of that great day of God Almighty.
>
> Behold, I come as a thief. Blessed is he that watcheth, and keepeth his garments, lest he walk naked, and they see his shame.
>
> And he gathered them together into a place called in the Hebrew tongue Armageddon. (Revelation 16:12–16)

Revelation 16:12–16 covers much that is extremely important for us to understand. First, the drying up of the Euphrates River is very significant as it has always been a natural boundary and barrier that helps protect Israel form her enemies. The Lord has often dried up water when he finds it necessary. The following are examples of such events: Exodus 14:21; Joshua 3:13–17; Isaiah 11:15–16, 19:5, 51:10; Jeremiah 50:28, 51:36; and Zechariah 10:11.

The drying up of the great river Euphrates will open up the way for the kings of the east to more easily get access to Israel, where they hope to accomplish their evil designs of finally exterminating Israel once and for all. The kings of the east are not the good guys; rather, they are the enemies of the Lord who are marching forth to destroy all good that will be remaining on the earth at that time. But to their surprise, this will be the final battle, and in the end, they will be the ones that are eliminated.

The three unclean spirits like frogs that will come out of the mouth of the dragon/beast and the mouth of the false prophet are nothing more than evil spirits and evil mortals who work for Satan. Satan is the designer of it all. All this is designed to deceive the people of the earth—anyone who will listen. Those who will be deceived are those who are not following the Lord and are not living His commandments.

As far as the spirits of devils working miracles, again these are designed to deceive the kings and leaders of the earth, so they will gather their forces for the final battle of evil against good (or Satan against God). These evil forces are real and we must know how to deal with them. The Lord warned us,

> For there shall arise false Christs, and false prophets, and shall shew great signs and wonders; insomuch that, if it were possible they shall deceive the very elect. (Matthew 24:24)

Again in latter day scripture, the Lord made it even clearer:

> Hearken, O ye elders of my church, and give ear to the voice of the living God; and attend to the words of wisdom which shall be given unto you, according as ye have asked and are agreed as touching the church, and the spirits which have gone abroad in the earth.
>
> Behold, verily I say unto you, that there are many spirits, which are false spirits, which have gone forth in the earth, deceiving the world.
>
> And also Satan hath sought to deceive you, that he might overthrow you. (D&C 50:1–3)

Elder Bruce R. McConkie stated, "And what greater miracle can these evil spirits perform, working as they always have through receptive mortals, than to indoctrinate men in all nations with that hate and lust for power which will cause them to assemble (in an age of atomic warfare!) with a view to the utter destruction of civilization? Then, as that great day of God Almighty arrives, and as the war of wars is being waged, Christ will come."[3]

Matthew, speaking about this time period, stated:

> And then shall many be offended, and shall betray one another, and shall hate one another.
>
> And many false prophets shall rise, and shall deceive many.
>
> And because iniquity shall abound, the love of many shall wax cold. (Matthew 24:10–12)

During this time faithful members of the Church have special callings, responsibilities, and duties to perform. Ours is to follow the Lord, live his commandments, and do all we can to help bring as many souls to him as possible. This means global missionary work:

> But he that shall endure unto the end, the same shall be saved. And this gospel of the kingdom shall be preached in all the world for a witness unto all nations; and then shall the end come. (Matthew 24:13–14)

The evil that will abound on the earth at this time will have great influence on the rulers of nations. Hatred will be at an all-time high and nation will be fighting against nation. The spirits of devils, working miracles, will go forth unto the kings of the earth and gather them to that great battle. This will be the final battle, the battle at Armageddon. It will be fought by many nations and armies of the earth and will be a worldwide conflict.

During the battle of Armageddon is when the Lord said he would come as a thief:

> Remember therefore how thou hast received and heard, and hold fast, and repent. If therefore thou shalt not watch, I will come on thee as a thief, and thou shalt not know what hour I will come upon thee. (Revelation 3:3)

We have been admonished to watch and be prepared for the Lord when he returns:

> And then they shall look for me, and behold, I will come; and they shall see me in the clouds of heaven, clothed with power and great glory; with all the holy angels; and he that watches not for me shall be cut off. (D&C 45:44).

We have also been warned that we should keep our garments spotless. To me this means to stay pure and stay away from sin and the evil of this world. It also means to keep our covenants we made in the temple:

> And may the Lord bless you, and keep your garments spotless, that ye may at last be brought to sit down with Abraham, Isaac, and Jacob, and the holy prophets who have been ever since the world began, having your garments spotless even as their garments are spotless, in the kingdom of heaven to go no more out. (Alma 7:25)

A number of years ago my wife and I had the opportunity to go to Israel and visit the area where the ancient city of Megiddo was. This area overlooks the vast plains where the last battle of Armageddon will be fought. This is the same area where many major battles have already been fought. The area is now made up of peaceful well-kept agricultural fields. But this peaceful picture will not continue, as this place is designated to be the place where Armageddon, the final battle, will be fought.

The sad thing is that the battle of Armageddon will not only be fought in Israel, but it will also be fought around the world. It will be a world war, since all nations will be affected by the evil of the day. The goal of Satan is not only the defeat of Israel, but also the destruction of all that is good—the Lord's work. The center will be Armageddon, but it will be a worldwide conflict and the vengeance of the Lord will be on all mankind that have joined the beast.

The Seventh Angel

The seventh angel will pour out his vial into the air. This will lead to wars around the world that will eventually overthrow Babylon:

> And the seventh angel poured out his vial into the air; and there came a great voice out of the temple of heaven, from the throne, saying, It is done. And there were voices, and thunders, and lightnings; and there was a great earthquake, such as was not since men were upon the earth, so mighty an earthquake, and so great. (Revelation 16:17–18)

The great voice out of the temple will be the voice of God the Father, saying it is done. This means it will be time for the final destruction of Babylon and all wickedness on the earth.

The best way to describe this time period is in the words of Elder Bruce R. McConkie: "This is the time when earth's land masses shall unite; when islands and continents shall become one land; when every valley shall be exalted and every mountain shall be made low; when the rugged terrain of today shall level out into a millennial garden; when the great deep shall be driven back into its own place in the north. It is no wonder that the earthquake shall exceed all others in the entire history of the world."[4] (See also D&C 133:21–25).

The earthquake described here will be the largest earthquake the world has ever known. This earthquake will level the mountains of the earth and put the world back in its original form. This earthquake will shake the entire globe all at once and everything will be affected and changed. At this time Christ will return in his glory:

> For thus saith the Lord of hosts; yet once, it is a little while, and I will shake the heavens, and the earth, and the sea, and the dry land; And I will shake all nations, and the desire of all nations shall come; and I will fill this house with glory, saith the Lord of hosts. (Haggai 2:6–7)

> And the great city was divided into three parts, and the cities of the nations fell: and great Babylon came in remembrance before God, to give unto her the cup of the wine of the fierceness of his wrath. And every island fled away, and the mountains were not found. (Revelation 16:19–20)

The great city, or Babylon, represents all the wicked and evil of the earth. The dividing of the city into three parts means the world is so wicked that it was fully ripe for the final destruction. The falling of the cities of the nations describes both the destruction by the earthquake and the falling and obliteration of the evil leaders of all the cities and nations of the earth. This will be when the entire earth will be cleansed and all wickedness will be wiped off the face of the earth:

> And thus, with the sword and by bloodshed the inhabitants of the earth shall mourn; and with famine, and plague, and earthquake, and the thunder of heaven, and the fierce and vivid lightning also, shall the inhabitants of the earth be made to feel the wrath, and indignation, and chastening hand of an Almighty God, until the consumption decreed hath made a full end of all nations. (D&C 87:6)

> And there fell upon men a great hail out of heaven, every stone about the weight of a talent: and men blasphemed God because of the plague of the hail; for the plague thereof was exceeding great. (Revelation 16:21)

The great hailstones will have an enormous devastating effect as they will probably be as big as basketballs or larger and weigh more than thirty pounds each. This will be just another plague to punish the evil of the earth. From this we know they will not humble themselves, but will again blaspheme God because of this terrible plague:

> And there shall be a great hailstorm sent forth to destroy the crops of the earth. And it shall come to pass, because of the wickedness of the world, that I will take vengeance upon the wicked, for they will not repent; for the cup of mine indignation is full; for behold, my blood shall not cleanse them if they hear me not. (D&C 29:16–17)

The battle of Armageddon, the last and final battle, will be a worldwide conflict. It will partially be brought about because of differences in religious beliefs. But the main reason it will occur is because the world has chosen iniquity:

> And if the time comes that the voice of the people doth choose iniquity, then is the time that the judgments of God will come upon you; yea, then is the time he will visit you with great destruction even as he has hitherto visited this land. (Mosiah 29:27)

The plagues that will be poured out will not cause the proud and wicked to repent, rather they will blaspheme God and continue to become even more evil, until they ultimately receive their final reward—eternal damnation.

This is the destiny the world has to look forward to.

So What Are We to Do?

I am glad you asked. Now is the time to

> Put on the whole armour of God, that ye may be able to stand against the wiles of the devil.
>
> For we wrestle not against flesh and blood, but against principalities, against powers, against the rulers of the darkness of this world, against spiritual wickedness in high places.
>
> Wherefore take unto you the whole armour of God, that ye may be able to withstand in the evil day, and having done all, to stand.
>
> Stand therefore, having your loins girt about with truth, and having on the breastplate of righteousness;
>
> And your feet shod with the preparation of the gospel of peace;
>
> Above all, taking the shield of faith, wherewith ye shall be able to quench all the fiery darts of the wicked.
>
> And take the helmet of salvation, and the sword of the Spirit, which is the word of God;
>
> Praying always with all prayer and supplication in the Spirit, and watching thereunto with all perseverance and supplication for all saints. (Ephesians 6:11–18)

Notes

1. United States Environmental Protection Agency, *Global Warming,* 6 April 2001.

2. Ezra Taft Benson, "The Law of Chastity," Brigham Young University Devotional, Provo, Utah, 13 October 1987.

3. Bruce R. McConkie, *The Millennial Messiah: The Second Coming of the Son of Man* (Salt Lake City: Deseret Book, 1982), 393.

4. Ibid.

3

The Plague of Apathy

Apathy is a major contributor to every scourge we face. While people are dying in regions hit by natural disaster, wealthy nations burn millions of tons of food each year to maintain high prices for their farm produce. The "haves"—the richest one fifth of the people in the world—consume 86 percent of all goods and services, while the poorest one-fifth consumes only 1.3 percent. The three richest people in the world have combined assets of more than the gross domestic product of the forty-eight least developed countries in the world. The world's 225 richest people, have a combined wealth of over one trillion dollars. This is equal to the annual income of the poorest 47 percent of the entire world's population. Of the 4.4 billion people in developing countries, nearly three-fifths lack access to safe sewers, a third have no access to clean water, a quarter do not have adequate housing, and a fifth have no access to health services of any kind.[1]

This is happening while Americans and Europeans spend 17 billion dollars a year on pet food. This is 4 billion dollars more than the estimated annual additional funds needed to provide basic health and nutrition for all the hungry in the world.[2]

What if we actually demanded that our resources be used toward helping rather than maiming mankind? President Eisenhower observed in a national speech to the American people in 1953, "Every gun that is made, every warship launched, every rocket fired signifies in the final sense, a theft from those who hunger and are not fed, those who are cold and are not clothed."[3] In the book *Countdown to Armageddon,* the writer observed that all those who died from starvation in the 1990s could have been saved for the price of ten stealth bombers.[4] This year alone, over four million people will die from starvation.[5]

Of course, we all know that the cost of war is outrageous. The Gulf war alone cost a half billion dollars a day. Fighter planes cost around $25 million each. One Tomahawk missile costs about $1.3 million. Each air-to-air missile is about $800,000. Tank shells cost between $2,000 to $36,000 each. Should we be more involved in how our money is spent? How much food could this provide to the hungry and starving? If a small fraction of what goes into the military were put into feeding the hungry of the world, there would be no hunger.

The Disintegration of Responsibility

One unfortunate by-product of personal apathy is the disintegration of fiscal responsibility. When those in responsible positions are more interested in gain than in the good of their country, terrible things happen. But are we not all to one degree or another giving up an important social responsibility in pursuit of personal gratification? Is apathy an epidemic as far-reaching in its consequences as greed?

While in Russia, I observed daily how money that should have gone into public preservation instead went into the pockets of men who continue to be more interested in personal gain than the welfare of their nation. The livestock barns in Russia that were previously full in the early 1990s are now for the most part empty and decaying. Most of the tractor and combine factories that previously provided farm equipment to large state-owned farms have either been abandoned and are decaying, or are producing non-farm equipment. The farm equipment that is used is rapidly aging and not being replaced. One large state farm that I visited had forty combines, but only fourteen of them were functional. All the others were being robbed for their parts.

Throughout the former Soviet Union, we see young people abandoning the large government-owned farms because wages are so low. Wages are presently between $8 and $50 per month—plus whatever the workers can steal from the farm. The only people left to run the state farms are the old, and they—like the farm machinery—are also decaying rapidly because of excessive consumption of tobacco and alcohol, and very inadequate health care.

Vast areas of land that previously produced grain crops are now producing such things as sunflowers for oil to be sent abroad. Many hectares have simply been abandoned. Much of the farmland throughout the former Soviet Union has gone to weeds. In addition, thousands of hectares of land in Russia, Kazakhstan, and elsewhere in the former Soviet Union can no longer produce agricultural crops because the soil has become so polluted with industrial chemicals that it will never be suited for agricultural production again.

I see some very hard times ahead. By that, I mean that large-scale famine in the former Soviet Union could occur within a few years. The price of apathy is huge.

Then I thought about America, "a land of plenty." And I thought, "yes, but for how long?" The average American farmer is now over fifty-five years old. Youth are no longer staying on the farms, as the wages are too low, the hours too long, and the work too hard. Parents and teachers no longer try to persuade their kids to stay on the family farms. Who cares where the food comes from? Aren't the stores full of anything we need or want?

There is not even an organization called "Future Farmers of America" anymore. There is only a very weak remnant called FFA. The program has the letters of Future Farmers of America, but it does not mean Future Farmers of America, as those responsible for the program are afraid the word "farmers" will drive students away. The major subject matter taught has moved from farming and "How to become a successful farmer," to such things as "Ecology," "Greenhouse Management," "Forestry," "Ornamental Horticulture," and a little agribusiness—only topics that might interest kids. The program no longer produces a generation that knows how to or even wants to feed the nation. In addition, throughout the country, schools are dropping the FFA program as fast as they can. The same thing has happened to the 4-H program. There is no longer an organization designed to produce a future generation of farmers who are ready to feed the people of America and the world! This is sad but true. So? Should that be of any concern to me?

We are losing thousands of family farms throughout the United States each year. No industry can stay in business without a profit. The cost-price squeeze is now choking many of them. The family farm system of agriculture is now facing eradication. For the past 25 years we have witnessed an ever-increasing number of farm bankruptcies, foreclosures, and evictions. These, in turn, have led to unbelievable stress, alcoholism, divorce, family violence, and even suicides. We are now witnessing the economic and social structure of rural America crumbling as more and more of our food supply is taken over by corporate agribusiness, the ultimate merchants of greed.

The Burden of Farmers

Joel prophesied of the calamities that will envelop the earth, including the United States, just prior to the "day of the Lord." He told of the hunger, famine, wars, plagues, and all other forms of misery that will inflict the inhabitants because of gross wickedness that will reign on the earth. Joel showed the consequences of greed, pride, and other forms of evil that will shroud the earth at this time.

> He hath laid my vine waste, and barked my fig tree: he hath made it clean bare, and cast it away; the branches thereof are made white. . . .
>
> The field is wasted, the land mourneth; for the corn is wasted: the new wine is dried up, the oil languisheth.
>
> Be ye ashamed, O ye husbandmen; howl, O ye vinedressers, for the wheat and for the barley; because the harvest of the field is perished.
>
> The vine is dried up, and the fig tree languisheth; the pomegranate tree, the palm tree also, and the apple tree, even all the trees of the field, are withered: because joy is withered away from the sons of men. . . .
>
> Alas for the day! for the day of the Lord is at hand, and as a destruction from the Almighty shall it come.
>
> Is not the meat cut off before our eyes, yea, joy and gladness from the house of our God?
>
> The seed is rotten under their clods, the garners are laid desolate, the barns are broken down; for the corn is withered.
>
> How do the beasts groan! the herds of cattle are perplexed, because they have no pasture; yea, the flocks of sheep are made desolate.
>
> O Lord, to thee will I cry: for the fire hath devoured the pastures of the wilderness, and the flame hath burned all the trees of the field.
>
> The beasts of the field cry also unto thee: for the rivers of waters are dried up, and the fire hath devoured the pastures of the wilderness. (Joel 1:7, 10–12, 15–20)

These things are now happening and getting worse each and every day throughout the world. Appalling hunger and famine exist in many parts of the world including Africa, the Middle East, South and Central America, much of Asia, and so on. More and more nations of the earth cannot feed their citizens. Wickedness and all forms of evil are bringing wars to many of these nations, which is greatly accelerating the hunger, famine, and suffering of millions in those parts of the world.

For over a decade, I witnessed the steady decline of agriculture throughout the former Soviet Union. The orchards disappeared, the grain fields diminished, and the barns emptied, which are now decaying and tumbling down. The herds of cattle, sheep, and other livestock are mostly gone and those remaining are perplexed, because of lack of feed. Yes, the husbandmen have also abandoned their post; only the old and decaying farmworkers remain on the large government farms in what was once the breadbasket of the world. Soon famine will stalk that part of the world as well.

Agriculturally speaking, conditions in the United States are presently better than in much of the world, but American agriculture is in grave danger and declining at lightning speed. Eight hundred acres of prime agricultural land are lost each and every day to urban and industrial expansion. Family farms are disappearing at the rate of 16,000 farms every year, because farm families can no longer make a living on their farms. Therefore young people are not going into farming. The average age of American farmers is now over fifty-five years. Lack of water is resulting in drought conditions over an increasing portion of the nation's prime cropland. Corporate agribusiness is rapidly taking over what farming is left in the United States. When corporate agribusiness has mined the soil and gleaned all they can, they too will abandon the post, and there will be no one left to produce our food. World famine has been prophesied since the beginning. For all these reasons and many more, global famine will soon be a reality.

What if the farmers who are presently working harder than many other groups of people and getting paid the least should decide to quit and walk off their farms? Oh yes, this could happen. In fact, it is happening right now. As more and more farmers are hit with a cost-price squeeze, they are being forced off their land. More of them are realizing that for every loaf of bread that consumers pay two dollars, farmers only receive twelve cents. The middlemen get the rest. In the past ten years, we have lost 155,000 farms. That is an average of 16,000 farms per year.[6]

If we are losing 16,000 farms each year, then how many farms are left in the United States? The American Farm Bureau stated in August 1999 there are 1.9 million farms left. The scary thing about this number is that this is the lowest number of farms in the US since 1850.[7]

It is getting harder and harder for farmers to stay in business. Following are some facts that could lead to famine in this country:

1. Farmers' share of each food dollar has dropped steadily over the past forty years, from 41 cents in 1950 to only 20 cents in 1999.[8]
2. The average price farmers received for corn in 1999 was the lowest in twenty-five years.[9]
3. Since 1985, farm prices have dropped steadily for commodities such as corn, wheat, and soybeans. Currently, these prices are 35–50 percent lower than they were fifteen years ago.[10]
4. In 1998, farmers earned an average of only $7,000 per year from their farming operations.[11]
5. Most family farmers must work jobs off the farm just to make ends meet; 88 percent of the average farm operator's household income comes from off-the-farm sources.[12]
6. Of all the occupations in America, farming is facing the greatest decline.[13]
7. Again I would like to emphasize that there are only 1.91 million farms remaining in the United States. This is the lowest number of farmers America has had since 1850.[14]
8. Between 1993 and 1997, the number of mid-sized family farms dropped by 74,440.[15]
9. Only 8 percent of all American farmers are under the age of thirty-five.[16]
10. In 1970, there were approximately 900,000 hog farmers in the United States; by 1997, there were only 139,000.[17]
11. Since 1986, the number of hog operations has declined by 72 percent—a loss of over 247,500 operations. Of the remaining hog operations, 2 percent control nearly half of all hog inventory.[18]
12. Ninety percent of the nations poultry production is now controlled by ten companies.[19]

There are four things that have been driving farmers out of business over the past fifteen plus years. First, where there is no profit, no business can long survive. Farmers have been hit with a cost-price-squeeze that is driving thousands of them off their land. Because of the cheap food policy our government has taken, consumers have had cheap food, but farmer's costs have continued to rise while their income has remained the same. This cannot continue. Government controls must be fair and equitable or older farmers will continue to leave their farms in great numbers while young people will not, and simply cannot, go into a business that provides no profit.

Up until January 2002, the second thing that caused the downfall of family farms was again the irresponsibility of government. Taxes were unrealistic and unbearable for farmers. The most unfair tax of all was the Inheritance Tax, which proved to be the kiss of death to American family farms. Fortunately for farmers and the American people in general, in January 2002, President Bush's "Economic Growth and Tax Relief Reconciliation Act" of 2001 was implemented. This new legislation will once again make it possible for young farmers to take over their parent's farm. Until 2002, farmers had no tax relief since Ronald Regan's historic tax cut in the early 1980s. Since President Regan's tenure, conditions have worsened each year until the Bush administration showed this outstanding foresight and leadership. Now there will be no inheritance tax on the first $1,000,000 value of the farm. This should once again provide a way for young farmers to take over their parent's farm. Whether they can make a profit on it is still another matter though.

Until 2002, inheritance tax placed an outrageous tax on property that was transferred from one generation to the next. This was a tax on the value of the farm and had to be paid by the son when he took over the farm. This tax was 40 percent of the property value if it was $300,000 or less and 60 percent for everything over $600,000. This meant that if a father gave his son the family farm worth $200,000, the son was immediately stuck with an $80,000 tax bill to Uncle Sam. If the son wanted to continue farming he had to get a loan to pay the taxes. Remember the average American farmers are only making $7,000 per year off that farm. How many kids today want to take on that kind of misery, so they can work harder than any other group of people in the country and make the least money?

One day when I was farming in Wisconsin, I told my sons: "Just think, someday all this will be yours." In unison, they all said that if I gave them the farm, they would turn me in for child abuse. None of them wanted the farm, and none of them became farmers and I cannot blame them. There was no profit in farming then, and it is even worse now.

Inheritance taxes were killing the family farms of America. And it can happen again. The Economic Growth and Tax Relief Reconciliation Act of 2001 is not legislation that will last indefinitely. In 2011, conditions will automatically be reinstated to the year 2000 level under the "Sunset Provision" of the law. Basically, what Congress did was to pass a law to make them on the surface appear to have repealed estate tax, but in reality they have left it up to three more elections and three more congresses to finalize the repeal—and if the future congresses do not finalize the bill, it is automatically reinstated in 2011 to the 2000 year status.

We still have property taxes. This is another tax that is killing the farmers. Again, I speak from personal experience. Property tax on our farm was $7,238 during the last year we farmed. This is not an equitable tax. Landowners are taxed while renters pay nothing. Yet their children go to the same schools, drive on the same highways, and use the same public facilities as owners.

The next thing that is driving farmers out of business is the North American Free Trade Agreement, (NAFTA). The Washington Post July 10th, 1999 states, "Trade agreements such as the North American Free Trade Agreement encourage farm concentration and allow unfair competition from Canadian and some European countries, which heavily subsidize farms." On July 1, 1999, the U.S. Department of Commerce found that Canada was exporting cattle to the U.S. at below-market prices and then subsidizing their own farmers. This type of unfair competition is greatly hurting American farmers.[20]

All this has happened while the income of farmers has basically remained the same since 1981. The average American farmer works over sixty hours per week, earning $6.66 per hour or $400 per week for a total of $20,800 per year. And the very sad part is that the average American farmer only nets $7,000 from a farming operation. Most farm families must work jobs off the farm just to make ends meet. Eighty-eight percent of the average farm operator's household income comes from off-the-farm sources. And there is usually more than one in the family that is working to bring in this income.[21] The average American high school graduate earns about $9,000 more than a farmer and only works forty hours per week.[22]

In 1981, the average cost of health insurance was $87 per month for a family. And there were no deductibles. Today, health insurance costs a family close to $600 per month. If a farmer paid $600 a month, that would be $7,200 a year, or $200 more than he nets off his entire farm for the year. The only way a farmer can afford any health insurance is to get a policy with a very high deductible, and then the farmer will have to pay for all office calls, medication, and everything else up to that deductible amount. And a $1000 deductible policy will still cost close to $400 per month. Or a $2,500 deductible policy will cost about $300 per month.[23] Since farmers are self-employed, if they want health insurance they have to pay all the costs themselves. Needless to say, many farmers cannot afford health insurance even at the higher deductible rates.

Farmers' ages have something to do with high health insurance costs as well. The average American farmer is now over 55 years old. Today, it costs the average person over 65 years of age $12,000 per year per person for health care services. And those over 85, (the fastest growing age group in our country) average $20,000 per year. Each year, many farms are lost because farmers cannot pay health care costs, so they lose their farms in order to prolong their lives.

Large corporations that have no love or regard for the land, environment, or any part of the ecosystem are replacing family farms that have traditionally been the stewards of the land. Unlike the traditional family farms, it is not the purpose of corporate agribusiness to feed people, or insure the long lasting sustainable husbandry, maintenance, or care of the land. Rather, their sole purpose is to mine the soil of all its natural resources in order to create a profit for now, while disregarding future generations. Corporate greed has moved into every industry in the United States, but the two most notorious merchants of greed are corporate agribusiness and the health care industry.

The only concern of corporate agribusiness is how much they can enrich themselves. This is happening at a time when more and more of the needy are going hungry. This is occurring in a world that has more than enough food to feed everyone on this planet. Corporate agribusiness has made it impossible for the natural, wholesome, healthy environment of family farming and agriculture to continue. Their greed is rapidly changing agriculture to agri-business, which is seriously jeopardizing our environment, the health and safety of food, and our future food supply. The merchants of greed are putting the world on the brink of global disaster.

This greed is leading to worldwide economic, political, social, and environmental chaos unlike anything seen in human history. This kind of greed along with a disregard for the environment and the entire ecosystem are some of the major things that could lead to the coming famine and pestilence prophesied of in the last days.

In addition, these large corporate farms have proven to be much less effective, as they are operated by disinterested workers instead of dedicated owners who are willing to put in long hours with no extra pay. Stockholders then shut down these same corporate farms when profit margins are not adequate. Corporate agribusiness discards family farmers as useless excess garbage, causing thousands of them to forever leave the family farm each year. Corporate agribusiness has no concern for workers, as they are considered then to be no more than rented slaves that will be replaced by technology whenever possible.

How long can the American farmer put up with this greed, and the greed from other sources including the American Tax System that is making it impossible for him to make a living? How long can farmers afford to keep providing America with cheap food? When they are no longer profitable, who will produce the nation's vegetables, grains, fruit, meat, milk, poultry, and so forth? How long will it be before they throw in the towel and say good riddance? How long will it be until large-scale famine hits this land for all the many reasons? I believe it is only a question of time. (See Chapter 9.)

Loss of Land to Feed the People

A further complication to keeping the world fed is that each and every day, vast areas of agricultural land all over the world are permanently taken out of food production because of urban sprawl. In the United States, we lose eight hundred acres every day to urban sprawl. The main problem is that agricultural land is worth more for development projects than it is for farming. In many areas of the United States, homebuilders pay $10,000 and more per acre for land. This same land is worth about one to two thousand dollars per acre as farmland. Each and every day, more and more of the very best farmland that feeds the people of this nation—and much of the world—is lost forever. I call this the "Shrinking Fields Pheomenon"—a very real problem. In the next five years, there will be 400 million more people to feed, yet each day more and more of the world's best cropland is permanently lost to urban and industrial expansion; each year, an area about one kilometer wide stretching from San Francisco to New York is permanently lost to food and agricultural production.

Unfortunately, this urbanization of important farmlands is happening in every country around the world. For example, in China, five percent of China's cropland was lost in only six years to urban expansion. Yet Chinese officials plan to establish six hundred new cities in the next fourteen years. Java lost more than twenty thousand hectares of cropland to urban and industrial expansion in 1994 alone. More than three hundred thousand acres of California's prime cropland has been permanently lost since 1984. In the United States, more than eight hundred acres of prime agricultural land is lost each and every day to urban and industrial expansion. Each year the United States permanently loses an area about one kilometer wide stretching from San Francisco to New York that is forever gone for food and agricultural production.

In addition to land lost to urban and industrial expansion, much more land has been lost to degradation because of erosion, mismanagement, and salinization. Kazakhstan, the world's eleventh largest country and one of the leading grain producers, has lost 24 percent of its grain land to erosion and chemical pollution since the mid-1980s. On a worldwide basis, an area equal to two Canadas has permanently been removed from production since the end of WWII. In the United States, one third of our nation's topsoil has been permanently lost since 1945.

All this comes at a time when over 800 million people live in uncertainty of their next meal. And 185 million preschool children suffer mental or physical maldevelopment because of malnutrition. And the world population is expected to grow by 80 million people each year for the next twenty-five years. Between 1990 and 2020, global demand for grain is projected to increase by 55 percent, by 75 percent for livestock products, and by 50 percent for roots and tubers.[24]

Yields are leveling off and declining as plants have reached their biological limits of production, despite the addition of more water, fertilizer, herbicides, and pesticides. In fact, misuse and overuse of these inputs has led to global environmental degradation and the depletion of water supplies.

In *The Miracle of Forgiveness,* President Kimball discusses the upcoming calamities for those who have not listened, and are not prepared:

The land will be barren (perhaps radioactive or dry from drought). The trees will be without fruit and the fields without verdure. There will be rationing and a scarcity of food, and sore hunger. No traffic will jam your desolate highways. Famine will stalk rudely through your doors and the ogre of cannibalism will rob you of your children and your remaining virtues will disintegrate. There will be pestilence uncontrollable. Your dead bodies will be piled upon the materialistic things you sought so hard to accumulate and save. There will be no protection against enemies. They that hate you shall reign over you. Your power your supremacy your pride in superiority will be broken. Heaven will not hear your pleadings nor earth bring forth its harvest. Your strength will be spent in vain as you plow and plant and cultivate. Your cities will be shambles; your churches in ruins. Your enemies will be astonished at the barrenness, sterility, and desolation of the land they had been told was so choice, so beautiful, and so fruitful. You shall have no power to stand before your enemies. Your people will be scattered among the nations as slaves and bondsmen. You will pay tribute and bondage, and fetters shall bind you.[25]

Notes

1. Kofi Annan, "Astonishing Facts," *New York Times News Service,* edited by "The Family." 1997–2001.

2. Ibid.

3. President Dwight D. Eisenhower, "The Chance for Peace,"April 16, 1953.

4. *Countdown to Armageddon,* "Famine," The Family 1997-1999.

5. Ibid.

6. Ag. Facts, "Number of U.S. Farms Continues to Drop," compiled from the LSU Ag. Center and the American Farm Bureau Federation, 2000.

7. Ibid.

8. USDA Economic Research Service.

9. John M. Dietrich, "Key indicators of the U.S. Farm Sector: A 25-year history with inflation adjustments," April 2000.

10. Ibid.

11. USDA Economic Research Service, "Agricultural Outlook" May 2000, Table 31.

12. Ibid.

13. Occupational Outlook Quarterly, Winter 1999/2000. U.S. Department of Labour.

14. 1997 Census of Agriculture, USDA National Agricultural Statistics Service.

15. "Farm and Land in Farms, Final Estimates 1993–1997," USDA National Agricultural Statistics Service.

16. "Quick Facts" brochure based on 1997 Census of Agriculture. USDA National Agricultural Statistics Service, February 1999.

17. Mark Drabenscott, "This Little Piggy Went to Market." *Economic Review,* Federal Reserve Bank, Kansas City, Vol. 83, No. 3, 1998, 79–97.

18. December 1998 Hogs and Pigs Report, USDA National Agricultural Statistics Service.

19. Susan Zakin, "Nonpoint Pollution: The Quiet Killer, Field and Stream," August 1999, 84–88.

20. Paul Bathgate, "Family Farms, Pers Family Farm," http://forensics.truman.edu/CoachingPage/Pers_family_farms.html, September 12, 2001.

21. USDA Economic Research Service, "Agricultural Outlook" May 2000, Table 31.

22. America's Career Information Network, "Highest paying Occupations" December 5, 2001.

23. Personal knowledge of the author.

24. David Seckler, Randolph Barker and Amarasinghe Upali. Consultative Group on International Agricultural Research (CGIAR) "Water Scarcity in the Twenty-First Century" International Journal of Water Resources Development. Washington D.C. March 17, 1999.

25. Spencer W. Kimball, *The Miracle of Forgiveness* (Salt Lake City: Bookcraft, 1969), 320–21.

4

The Plague of Pride and Greed

Pride

Pride is excessive self-esteem arising because of a person's possessions, position, class, or achievements. Pride causes one to seek the things of the world rather than the riches of eternity. "For all that is in the world, the lust of the flesh, and the lust of the eyes, and the pride of life, is not of the Father, but is of the world" (1 John 2: 16). Pride is the central causes of contention. "Only by pride cometh contention: but with the well advised is wisdom" (Proverbs 13:10). Pride is wickedness and those who are proud will be destroyed at the Second Coming of Christ.

> Pride goeth before destruction, and an haughty spirit before a fall. (Proverbs 16:18)

> For after today cometh the burning—this is speaking after the manner of the Lord—for verily I say, tomorrow all the proud and they that do wickedly shall be as stubble; and I will burn them up, for I am the Lord of Hosts; and I will not spare any that remain in Babylon. (D&C 64:24)

Pride and greed are included in all forms of man's inhumanity to man—government corruption, economic oppression, embargoes, and wars.

Greed

Greed: n. excessive, inordinate or rapacious desire, esp. for wealth or possessions.[1]

Greed, most simply stated, is nothing more than selfishness. We have come to this earth to be tested to see if we will seek the riches of eternity or the fleeting counterfeits of this earth. Greed is the covetous grasping for an unreasonable amount of the things of this world; it is a sin. "In thee have they taken gifts to shed blood; thou hast taken usury and increase, and thou hast greedily gained of thy neighbours by extortion, and hast forgotten me, saith the Lord God" (Ezekial 22:11).

Nephi described what greediness would yield in the end.

> And the angel spake unto me, saying: Behold the gold, and the silver, and the silks, and the scarlets, and the fine-twined linen, and the precious clothing, and the harlots, are the desires of this great and abominable church. And also for the praise of the world do they destroy the saints of God, and bring them down into captivity. (1 Nephi 13:8–9)

Modern revelation again reminds us to seek the riches of eternity rather than to greedily seek earthly things.

> Now, I, the Lord, am not well pleased with the inhabitants of Zion, for there are idlers among them; and their children are also growing up in wickedness; they also seek not earnestly the riches of eternity, but their eyes are full of greediness. (D&C 68:31)

> Seek not for riches but for wisdom, and behold, the mysteries of God shall be unfolded unto you, and then shall you be made rich. Behold, he that hath eternal life is rich. (D&C 6:7)

Greed is bringing this nation and the world to the point where the end is in sight. I believe that humans are the creators of most of the calamities that will befall mankind in the last days. As greed, speculation, and the worship of idols team up with pride and arrogance, worse sins will soon follow:

> Woe unto them! for they have gone in the way of Cain, and ran greedily after the error of Balaam for reward, and perished in the gainsaying of Core. (Jude 1:11)

> Perverse disputings of men of corrupt minds, and destitute of the truth, supposing that gain is godliness: from such withdraw thyself.
>
> But godliness with contentment is great gain.
>
> For we brought nothing into this world, and it is certain we can carry nothing out.

> And having food and raiment let us be therewith content.
>
> But they that will be rich fall into temptation and a snare, and into many foolish and hurtful lusts, which drown men in destruction and perdition.
>
> For the love of money is the root of all evil: which while some coveted after, they have erred from the faith, and pierced themselves through with many sorrows.
>
> But thou, O man of God, flee these things; and follow after righteousness, godliness, faith, love, patience, meekness.
>
> Fight the good fight of faith, lay hold on eternal life, whereunto thou art also called, and hast professed a good profession before many witnesses. (1 Timothy 6: 5–12)

In 1876 the *Deseret News* published an article quoting President John Taylor describing greed and what we as members should be devoting our lives to rather than the accumulation of earthly wealth:

> Now, then, we are gathered together to help, what to do? To look after our own individual interests? No. To accumulate wealth? No. To possess and wallow in the good things of this life? No, but to do the will of God and devote ourselves, our talents and abilities, our intelligence and influence in every possible way to carry out the designs of Jehovah and help to establish peace and righteousness upon the earth. This, as I understand it, is what we are here for, and not to attend to our own individual affairs and let God and his kingdom do as they please. We are all interested in the great latter-day work of God, and we all ought to be co-workers therein.[2]

Corporate Greed

A plague that is most alarming in America today is "corporate greed." Most Americans have little knowledge of how pervasive corporate greed really is and how our political and economic system works. This is partially because corporate greed is often underreported, since these same large corporate conglomerates own newspapers, television networks, radio stations, and magazines. Many people do not understand the role "big money" plays in political and economic decisions that we are ultimately forced to live with.

It is easy to see greed in this nation. Consider the American pharmaceutical drug companies. The American people pay by far the highest prices in the world for prescription drugs. Many, if not most of the same drugs sold in the United States by American drug companies are sold abroad at a fraction of the price they are sold for in the United States. As a result, millions of our citizens suffer, and some die, because they are unable to afford the medicine they need.[3]

This happens, while year after year, drug companies continue to be some of the most profitable industries in the world. Last year alone, their profits exceeded $30 billion. Each year the cost of prescription drugs continues to climb. Last year alone, the cost of prescription drugs rose by 17 percent. This is happening at a time when greed is causing elderly citizens to cut their dosages in half, or go without, yet nine top executives of U.S. pharmaceutical corporations were given $890 million in stock options. This was on top of the $169.9 million in wages, bonuses and other compensations these executives had already received.[4]

You might ask, how are the drug companies able to get away with such gross greed? By paying millions in campaign contributions, lobbying, and advertising fees. They have chosen greed over the health of the American people. This greed is unfortunately producing a country with haves and the have-nots—another example of the Nephite disease at epidemic level, which is bringing this nation down.

In 1980, CEO compensation was forty-two times that of the average worker. In 2000, it was 531 times. This is a winner-take-all philosophy that is unacceptable in American society, especially at a time when teamwork is being extolled as the key to higher productivity and company success and all employees are putting in long hours at the office or on the line. The size of CEO compensation is simply out of hand. Yet in Germany, CEOs make only about twenty-one times the pay of their average workers. And in Japan about sixteen times as much.[5]

Over the past twenty years in the United States—in both good times and bad—workers' wages have declined as compared with the cost of living even though productivity and corporate profits have increased. Profitability has continued to increase because companies are cutting jobs, reducing or eliminating benefits, hiring part-time people, and moving production abroad. Today, twice as many middle-aged American workers now permanently lose their jobs as they did two decades ago.

As this is happening, "welfare" payments from our government to these corporations continue to skyrocket. You will be happy to learn that just before the three top executives of Enron made off with $560 million, as they abandoned their sinking ship, leaving 12,000 employees drowning, we, the American tax payers, gave Enron a check for $254 million as part of their so-called "economic stimulus plan."[6]

It is sad to see how many American corporations are moving their production facilities to foreign lands, because they can hire workers there at a fraction of what they pay here, and there is no benefit package to worry about. Yet the cost of their products continues to increase each year. A good example of this is IBM. They recently announced a new round of job cuts; and more than five thousand jobs will be lost in the United States since the company is moving two of its processing plants to China. And two years ago, despite record breaking profits and a huge pension fund surplus, IBM cut pension and retirement health benefits for workers and curtailed salaries. As this was happening, the CEO received $176 million in total compensation and stock options over the past few years. And yet with all the misery this company is causing its workers and the American people, it is possible for IBM to receive up to $1.4 billion of our tax payers dollars in corporate welfare this year.[7]

Now is the time for the American people to get on the ball and be more careful as to whom we vote into office. The greed factor has definitely affected people in all areas of government as well as corporations. We, the American taxpayers, are left holding the bag. Or I should say, we are the ones emptying our wallets to pay for greed and corruption.

I hope this will rekindle in each of us a dedication to have a year's supply of food on hand, as we have been counseled by Church leaders for many years. (See chapter 9.)

The second mega-beast in the greed trade is the health care industry. Combine managed care for profit and service providers with insurance companies, and what do you get? HMOs, or huge merchants of greed, that are in business for profit, "nothing else." In essence we get the shaft. They get the green, at the expense of all of us. What do the poor and uninsured get? They get nothing but pain, misery, and death.

The managed care-for-profit HMOs are even greedier than the corporate agribusinesses. In essence they have a license to steal. And they are expert at their trade of stealing from the poor and giving to the rich—themselves. "Who being past feeling have given themselves over unto lasciviousness, to work all uncleanness with greediness" (Ephesians 4:19).

How do they operate? The HMO insists that members can only see a primary physician whom they (the HMO) designate for all your medical needs. This corporate flunky is nothing more than a company gatekeeper.

He must approve all care. If you need a specialist, this gatekeeper has to refer you and can deny needed care. The fact is that HMOs are notorious for paying bonuses to those doctors for providing a minimum of care, while doctors that provide more than what the HMO thinks is needed are penalized. HMOs have even been known to put gag rules in place to stop the doctor from discussing alternative treatments outside of their HMO. Yes, greed and money is the name of their game.

HMO executives are paid large bonuses for controlling costs. This means decisions are made on profits, not on patient needs. If a patient who does not have insurance enters such a facility, they are simply out of luck. This recently happened to a friend of mine.

He had eaten some chicken and it got caught in his throat. He was having great difficulty breathing and was simply dying. He drove to the hospital in the town where he lives and asked them to remove it. The first question asked was, "Do you have insurance?" He did not, as he had recently returned home from a mission and did not yet have any. They said, "We cannot treat you!" Remember, he was dying. They told him to go to another city. He drove to the second city by himself and, with great difficulty, finally found the hospital.

With gasping speech he explained the problem to them; they asked him, "And do you have insurance?" When he said he did not, they said that they did not have anyone on duty that could take care of him. Instead, they said, "Why don't you go to another town?" It was twenty-seven miles away. By the time he got there he was gasping for air and had little time left. That facility also asked about his insurance, but reluctantly treated him as they could see he was dying. But they made sure he could pay before they would treat him. The man did not receive any anesthetics, as he knew he could not afford them, and he knew he could not afford to stay in the hospital that night, so he just had the chicken removed from his throat. The simple procedure took less than fifteen minutes.

The man lived, but the fifteen-minute procedure of removing the lodged piece of chicken from his throat cost him more than $2,000, all the money he had and much more. An interesting sidenote is that the same thing happened to him twice while he was on his mission in another country. The first time the total cost of the procedure was $25; the second time was in another city, and the total cost was just $4. When he received the bill for the procedure in the US, he noticed that all three hospitals were a division of the first place he went in his hometown. This is not health care; it is greed in its worst form!

> So are the ways of every one that is greedy of gain; which taketh away the life of the owners thereof. (Proverbs 1:19)

> Yea, they are greedy dogs which can never have enough, and they are shepherds that cannot understand: they all look to their own way, every one for his gain, from his quarter. (Isaiah 56:11)

The problems go on and on with the health care providers in the United States. These evils all stem from greed. This greed has made it so the poor have no protection. This class distinction will eventually lead to class warfare and violence that will ultimately bring this nation to its knees. (See chapter 8.)

I know this is very blunt, but it is time someone told it as it is. Elder Bruce R. McConkie also made a very strong statement when he said:

> Because of iniquity and greed in the hearts of men, there will be depressions, famines, and a frantic search for temporal security—a security sought without turning to the Lord or obeying his precepts. We may expect to see the insatiable desire to get something for nothing result in further class legislation and more socialistic experiments by governments. Economic inequalities will certainly give rise to further class warfare and bickering. There will be riots, bloodshed, hunger, commotion, turmoil, and panics. These are all signs of the times.[8]

In the Doctrine and Covenants we read:

> And in that day shall be heard of wars and rumors of wars, and the whole earth shall be in commotion, and men's hearts shall fail them, and they shall say that Christ delayeth his coming until the end of the earth. And the love of men shall wax cold, and iniquity shall abound. (D&C 45:26–27)

"Iniquity shall abound" describes the direction our world is going. Crime of every sort has indeed infected the entire planet. Murder, robbery, rape, every form of sexual immorality, and all crimes against persons and property abound. Juvenile delinquency is a problem of substantial magnitude. We read daily of strikes, violence, and unrest in the labor market. This is the beginning of class warfare that is the result of greed, greed found in corporations and government. Greed is fueling strikes and labor problems that are rocking the entire economic world. This is causing anarchy, rebellion, and crime in many segments of society and, if it continues, could eventually overthrow the government.

There will soon be great tests for members of the Church. We must forgo the things of the world and look to the Lord. We must not get caught up in this greed that is now covering our land. We must not become a part of it. We must seek first the kingdom of God, not the stuff of this earth. We are being tested to see if we will seek the riches of eternity rather than the fleeting wealth of the world. Greediness, the grasping for unreasonable quantities of the things of the world, is sin.

In the October 1965 general conference, Elder Harold B. Lee spoke on the test that will come to members of the Church in the last days. In his talk he referred to the words of President Heber C. Kimball, who said:

> We think we are secure here in the chambers of the everlasting hills, . . . but I want to say to you, . . . the time is coming when we will be mixed up in these now peaceful valleys to that extent that it will be difficult to tell the face of a Saint from the face of an enemy to the people of God. Then, brethren, look out for the great sieve, for there will be a great sifting time, and many will fall; for I say unto you there is a test, a TEST, a TEST coming, and who will be able to stand?[9]

I believe the test is no longer "coming"; it is now here. We are beginning to experience the great sifting that has been prophesied. The sad thing is that many members of the Church are failing the test, because they are not following the counsel of the prophets and the commandments of the Lord. Pride and greed are causing many members to fall into Satan's trap, as they have become lovers of pleasure and the transitory things of the earth more than lovers of God. This is producing some very serious consequences for those who are choosing this bitter path. An example of this was recently published in newspapers around the world.

> Utah is again setting records as the country's bankruptcy capital. In one year one in every 38 households files for bankruptcy in Utah. It is an astounding number and, frankly an embarrassment to the state. It is hard to fathom why Utah, where we claim to exemplify the pioneer virtues of thrift, hard work and self-sufficiency, lead the nation in bankruptcies. The reality is we get into financial trouble because we want too much too fast; we borrow, borrow, borrow; and we are simply unwilling to live modestly, within our means. The keep-up-with-the-

Joneses syndrome is alive and well in Utah. It is perhaps more pronounced than anywhere in the country.[10]

As members of the Church we must come to the realization that now is the time to decide who we will serve. Our time is well illustrated in 2 Timothy, where Paul discusses the last days:

> This know also, that in the last days perilous times shall come.
> For men shall be lovers of their own selves, covetous, boasters, proud, blasphemers, disobedient to parents, unthankful, unholy,
> Without natural affection, trucebreakers, false accusers, incontinent, fierce, despisers of those that are good,
> Traitors, heady, highminded, lovers of pleasures more than lovers of God;
> Having a form of godliness, but denying the power thereof: from such turn away. (2 Timothy 3:1–5)

And further:

> For the time will come when they will not endure sound doctrine; but after their own lusts shall they heap to themselves teachers, having itching ears; And they shall turn away their ears from the truth, and shall be turned unto fables. (2 Timothy 4:3–4)

Nephi similarly warned of the same things:

> But behold, in the last days, or in the days of the Gentiles—yea, behold all the nations of the Gentiles and also the Jews, both those who shall come upon this land [America] and those who shall be upon other lands, yea, even upon all the lands of the earth, behold, they will be drunken with iniquity and all manner of abominations—And when that day shall come they shall be visited of the Lord of Hosts, with thunder and with earthquake, and with a great noise, and with storm, and with tempest, and with the flame of devouring fire. (2 Nephi 27:1–2)

We have learned more on the subject from modern revelation:

> Verily, verily, I say unto you darkness covereth the earth, and gross darkness the minds of the people, and all flesh has become corrupt before my face. (D&C 112:23)

> Ye hear of wars in foreign lands; but, behold, I say unto you, they

> are nigh, even at your doors, and not many years hence ye shall hear of wars in your own lands. (D&C 45:63)

Speculation

Speculation: n. engagement in business transactions involving considerable risk but offering the chance of large gains.[11]

Speculation is an evil that has taken hold of some members, and most do not even recognize it. This is one of Satan's best tools to use on unsuspecting members who consider themselves good and faithful. Speculation is running rampant in the Church. This false god then leads to other false gods that take them far from the only true and living God of the universe.

Members have been taught all their lives to live the commandments; and we know that:

> Behold, vengeance cometh speedily upon the inhabitants of the earth, a day of wrath, a day of burning, a day of desolation, of weeping, of mourning, and of lamentation; and as a whirlwind it shall come upon all the face of the earth, saith the Lord. (D&C 112:24)

But many members do not realize that the wrath of the Lord will begin with the members of the Church, because we know the law and the commandments:

> *And upon my house shall it begin,* and from my house shall it go forth, saith the Lord; First among those among you, saith the Lord, who have professed to know my name and have not known me, and have blasphemed against me in the midst of my house, saith the Lord. (D&C 112:25–26; emphasis added).

Speculation has taken over the hearts and minds of many members:

> He is proud, knowing nothing, but doting about questions and strifes of words, whereof cometh envy, strife, railings, evil surmisings, perverse disputings of men of corrupt minds, and destitute of the truth, *supposing that gain is godliness:* from such *withdraw thyself.* (1 Timothy 6:4–5; emphasis added)

Many members have fallen into the trap of supposing that gain is godliness. This is part of the Nephite disease that brought that nation to ruin, and it is what is tearing at the foundation of this nation at this time.

One of the first commandments we received in modern scripture was: "Seek not for riches but for wisdom, and behold, the mysteries of God shall be unfolded unto you, and then shall you be made rich. Behold he that hath eternal life is rich" (D&C 6:7). This scripture makes it very clear what our priorities should be. The Lord knows that we cannot serve two masters as He has told us in the past:

> No servant can serve two masters: for either he will hate the one, and love the other; or else he will hold to the one, and despise the other. Ye cannot serve God and mammon. (Luke 16:13)

At the beginning of this dispensation, the Lord gave great warnings against seeking for the things of this world without seeking first the kingdom of God. The Lord called those who seek for the riches of the world rather than eternal riches "idlers" and called this trait "greediness":

> Now, I, the Lord, am not well pleased with the inhabitants of Zion, for there are idlers among them; and their children are also growing up in wickedness; they also seek not earnestly the riches of eternity, but their eyes are full of greediness. (D&C 68:31)

The Book of Mormon gets right to the point and leaves no room for doubt as to where our time, talent, and labor should be devoted.

> But the laborer in Zion shall labor for Zion; for if they labor for money they shall perish. (2 Nephi 26:31)

Almost as soon as the Church was restored, the spirit of speculation began to creep in and cause people to make a choice between God and mammon. It is sad to see people who had been leaders in the Church let go of the iron rod and seek after the stuff of this world, rather than the eternal riches in the kingdom of God.

In the mid-1830s, there was great speculation throughout the nation, which included real estate and personal property of all kinds. This spirit of speculation affected many members of the Church as well. It started in Kirtland when leading brethren switched their devotion from the Lord to speculation for the things of this earth. When they got involved in speculation, they spent their time and talent on speculation rather than building up the kingdom of God as they had been called and set apart to do. The results of speculation among the members concluded in greed, faultfinding, dissension, and apostasy. Members who were involved in speculation were affected by all the foul powers of earth and hell. These members formed secret combinations to overthrow the Church, and many of them fell so far that in the end they were involved in the murder of the Prophet Joseph Smith and others.

In 1837 there was a crash similar to the crash of 1929. The 1837 crash, like the crash of 1929, was brought on by the speculation of the day. During the crash, many members who were involved in speculation apostatized and tried to blame Joseph Smith for their losses, even though Joseph repeatedly warned them of the evils of speculation. These same members then turned to every evil way imaginable to obtain wealth by fraud and deception.

The problems the Church has suffered in this dispensation have come about because of disobedience, greed, and speculation by members. This includes the Ohio mobbings, the Missouri persecutions, the Martyrdom, the exodus to the West, and every other problem the Church has had. When members strive to serve mammon rather than God, they are left alone. The Saints were persecuted because of their disobedience. If they would have put their trust in the Lord, lived the commandments, and followed the Lord's Prophet, no power on earth or in hell could have affected them. This would have especially been true if the members would have followed the law of consecration. If they would have been obedient, none of the evils of speculation could have affected them.

Those who fell often held responsible offices and callings in the Church, but when they chose to follow Satan rather than the Lord, they were left alone to "kick against the pricks."

In the Doctrine and Covenants, we read:

> That the rights of the priesthood are inseparably connected with the powers of heaven, and that the powers of heaven cannot be controlled nor handled only upon the principles of righteousness.
>
> That they may be conferred upon us, it is true; but when we undertake to cover our sins, or to gratify our pride, our vain ambition, or to exercise control or dominion or compulsion upon the souls of the children of men, in any degree of unrighteousness, behold, the heavens withdraw themselves; the Spirit of the Lord is grieved; and when it is withdrawn, Amen to the priesthood or the authority of that man.
>
> Behold, ere he is aware, he is left unto himself, to kick against the pricks, to persecute the saints and to fight against God. (D&C 121:36–38)

Some members were left to themselves because of disobedience. They were too caught up in the things of the world and would not live the principles of the law of the celestial kingdom.

> But behold, they have not learned to be obedient to the things which I required at their hands, but are full of all manner of evil, and do not impart of their substance, as becometh saints, to the poor and afflicted among them;
>
> And are not united according to the union required by the law of the celestial kingdom;
>
> And Zion cannot be built up unless it is by the principles of the law of the celestial kingdom; otherwise I cannot receive her unto myself.
>
> And my people must needs be chastened until they learn obedience, if it must needs be, by the things which they suffer. (D&C 105:3–6)

By 1834 there was such a spirit of speculation in Kirtland that the members trampled under foot the higher law of consecration, and it was abandoned. Instead of the higher law, the Lord had to give the members a lesser law as he did the people who lived the law of Moses:

> And now, a commandment I give unto you concerning Zion, that you shall no longer be bound as a united order to your brethren of Zion, only on this wise— . . .
>
> The covenants being broken through transgression, by covetousness and feigned words—
>
> Therefore, you are dissolved as a united order with your brethren, that you are not bound only up to this hour unto them, only on this wise, as I said, by loan as shall be agreed by this order in council, as your circumstances will admit and the voice of the council direct. (D&C 104: 47, 52–53)

In other words, because of greed, covetousness, disobedience, hypocrisy, and self-justification, many members were left to kick against the pricks and received the lesser law. From then on, the greed of the members made it so the chastening of the Lord had to occur from time to time to reawaken them and to keep them focused on the kingdom of God rather than the stuff of this world. Because of greed, speculation, and idolatry, the early members were persecuted and driven from place to place until they finally arrived in Utah. I know that is not the way we like to hear it, but that is the way it was. As members we would like to believe that the saints were persecuted because they were holy and other people were the bad guys. In fact, ex-Mormons who had even been leaders in the Church and had completely fallen because of their greed and speculation persecuted the Saints often. These ex-members were responsible for inciting others against the Mormons. More often than not it was done for the purpose of obtaining more filthy lucre.[12]

When the Saints arrived in Utah, President Brigham Young preached against speculation. He wanted no speculation of lands so that the first settlers would not enrich themselves at the expense of those who would come later. His inspired leadership prevented speculation in the early days of Utah, and the entire Church began to prosper. The interest of the whole was their concern, and greed was seldom a part of those wonderful founders of the Church in Utah.

Then the spirit of speculation again began to creep in among the members. And again the Lord, through the hands of the government, the United States Army, and greedy merchants, chastened them.[13] Had they learned their lesson about greed and speculation? No. Apparently they needed another reminder.

Throughout the 1870s, the prophets warned against pride, speculation, and greed and taught the importance of working for the good of the whole rather than every man for himself. Then, in 1875, many entered into a covenant to observe the rules of the united order. Brigham Young, John Taylor, Wilford Woodruff, and Lorenzo Snow all were fervently behind this movement.[14]

By 1879 there were entire communities living the united order. There was satisfaction with all living the order. All fared alike; all were prospering. The Lord truly blessed them during this era. Much of Utah and even parts of Arizona had become a garden place where all enjoyed everything in common.[15]

But, by 1882 members were once again consumed with greed and speculation, and the spirit of Babylon again began to take over the hearts and minds of many members in Utah. Businessmen started gaining control of the cooperatives and replaced these cooperatives with private enterprises. The complete structure of the former cooperatives was changed, though they often kept the same name in order to take advantage of the name appeal. By the mid-1880s, most of the stock of the cooperatives had been sold to a few men who then controlled the operation, making them corporations that were run by major stockholders whose main concern was making as much profit as possible at the expense of the members. Utah had once again returned to Babylon. Basically, Zion reigned in Utah for about ten years.[16]

We can see that the only thing mankind has ever learned from history is that we have never learned anything from history.

Since the mid-1880s, Utah has not returned to a Zion society. Rather, greed and speculation in Utah has run rampant once again. Utah has become the center of the so-called "get-rich-quick" schemes. This form of speculation has taken over Utah to the point that this state is now known as the "Fraud Capitol of the USA." Experts have concluded the reason this is happening in Utah is because of greed, gullibility, and goodness among a people who associate worldly success with right and wrong.[17] Members have had to be warned to watch out for those who teach that accumulation of wealth is a sign of "blessedness." Timothy saw exactly what would happen in our day:

> Perverse disputings of men of corrupt minds, and destitute of the truth, supposing that gain is godliness: from such withdraw thyself. (1 Timothy 6:5)

All the Prophets since Paul have warned us to stay clear of such false salesmen and seek first the kingdom of God.

It appears that a growing number of Church members all over the world have corrupted the doctrines of the Church and are living as the Zoramites who Alma attempted to reclaim. We have modern-day Zoramites in the Church today:

> Now when Alma saw this his heart was grieved; for he saw that they were a wicked and a perverse people; yea, he saw that their hearts were set upon gold, and upon silver, and upon all manner of fine goods.
>
> Yea and he also saw that their hearts were lifted up unto great boasting, in their pride. . .
>
> Behold, O God, they cry unto thee, and yet their hearts are swallowed up in their pride. Behold, O God, they cry unto thee with their mouths, while they are puffed up, even to greatness, with the vain things of the world.
>
> Behold, O my God, their costly apparel, and their ringlets, and their bracelets, and their ornaments of gold, and all their precious things which they are ornamented with; and behold, their hearts are set upon them, and yet they cry unto thee and say—We thank thee, O

> God, for we are a chosen people unto thee, while others shall perish. (Alma 31:24–25, 27–28)

Because of greed, vanity and pride, modern-day Zoramites in the Church justify their arrogant feelings of superiority as they judge others, saying openly or in their minds that others are not "chosen" such as them or that they have brought on their own problems. They also justify their greed, vanity, and pride by saying that those who do not have what they have are lazy and less intelligent, or that they choose to be like that.

The problem today in the world is that more and more of the so-called "chosen people" and "chosen countries and governments" are choosing to look the other way when their brothers are in need. This is why we have all kinds of "-ites" or classes. This is why we will have class warfare in this country and throughout the world in a very few years. (See chapter 8).

What is ahead for the members of the Church? We know that God is an unchanging God; He is the same yesterday, today, and forever. He cannot be happy with the greed and other unrighteousness he sees in the Church at this time. Therefore we can expect some very tough chastening and trials ahead in the near future. No, all is not well in Zion. And if anyone tells you it is, they are very misinformed. Satan would like you to believe all is well in Zion—but he is a liar:

> For behold, at that day shall he rage in the hearts of the children of men, and stir them up to anger against that which is good. And others will he pacify, and lull them away into carnal security, that they will say: All is well in Zion: yea, Zion prospereth, all is well–and thus the devil cheateth their souls, and leadeth them away carefully down to hell. (2 Nephi 28:20–21)

Heber C. Kimball knew that all would not be well in the Church, and he did not mince any words in describing the final results of this path:

> After a while the gentiles will gather by the thousands to this place, and Salt Lake City will be classed among the wicked cities of the world. A spirit of speculation and extravagance will take possession of the Saints, and the results will be financial bondage. Persecution comes next and all true Latter-day Saints will be tested to the limit. Many will apostatize and other will be still not knowing what to do. The Saints will be put to tests that will try the integrity of the best of them.[18]

Idols

Idols: n. an image of a deity other than God. Any person or thing regarded with blind admiration, adoration or devotion. A false conception or notion; fallacy.[19]

> Thou shalt have no other gods before me. Thou shalt not make unto thee any graven image, or any likeness of any thing that is in heaven above, or that is in the earth beneath, or that is in the water under the earth. (Exodus 20:3–4; also see Deuteronomy 5:7–8 and Mosiah 12:35–36.

I believe the Lord made this the first of the Ten Commandments because it is the most important to him. If it is the most important to him, then it should be the most important to us also. The Lord emphasized the importance of this commandment when he said: "And thou shalt love the Lord thy God with all thine heart, and with all thy soul, and with all thy might" (Deuteronomy 6:5). And then he went on to reiterate the second part of the first commandment: "Ye shall not go after other gods, of the gods of the people which are round about you; For the Lord thy God is a jealous God among you lest the anger of the Lord thy God be kindled against thee, and destroy thee from off the face of the earth" Deuteronomy 6:14–15).

What kinds of false gods and idols do people worship today? Isaiah described our day when he discussed the false gods and idols that people would worship in the last days:

> Their land also is full of silver and gold, neither is there any end of their treasures; their land is also full of horses, neither is there any end of their chariots [automobiles]: Their land also is full of idols; they worship the work of their own hands, that which their own fingers have made. (Isaiah 2:7–8)

Nephi discussed a pattern that we see over and over again throughout the history of the world:

> But wo unto the rich, who are rich as to the things of the world. For because they are rich they despise the poor, and they persecute the meek, and their hearts are upon their treasures; Wherefore, their treasure is their god. And behold, their treasure shall perish with them also. (2 Nephi 9:30)

I really like the way that Jeremiah put it:

> As the partridge sitteth on eggs, and hatcheth them not; so he that getteth riches, and not by right, shall leave them in the midst of his days, and at his end shall be a fool. (Jeremiah 17:11)

We cannot take any idols with us. It is sad to see a world that is fighting for these false gods that only turn to our condemnation in the end.

We can also appreciate the straightforwardness of President Ezra Taft Benson as he addressed the worship of modern-day idols:

> Our affections are often too highly placed upon the paltry perishable objects. Material treasures of earth are merely to provide us, as it were, room and board while we are here at school. It is for earthly possessions in their proper place. Yes, this is but a place of temporary duration. We are here to learn the first lesson toward exaltation—obedience to the Lord's gospel plan.[20]

In another address, President Ezra Taft Benson asks us a very pointed question: "Are we too much bound up in the affairs of the world–obsessed with secular measuring sticks—gauging our deeds by whether or not they have brought us praise, honor, esteem, profits? Do we seek wealth, honor, and esteem as though they were ends in themselves, thus putting us at cross purposes with God because we become more attached to the material than to the spiritual?"[21]

The Lord speaking about our day said:

> They seek not the Lord to establish his righteousness, but every man walketh in his own way, and after the image of his own god, whose image is in the likeness of the world, and whose substance is that of an idol, which waxeth old and shall perish in Babylon, even Babylon the great, which shall fall. (D&C 1:16)

In 1976, President Spencer W. Kimball, speaking about the "False Gods We Worship," described the conditions the world would be in because of idol worship:

> Few men have ever knowingly and deliberately chosen to reject God and his blessings. Rather, we learn from the scriptures that because the exercise of faith has always appeared to be more difficult than relying on things more immediately at hand, carnal man has tended to transfer his trust in God to material things. Therefore, in all ages

> when men have fallen under the power of Satan and lost the faith, they have put in its place a hope in the "arm of flesh" and in "gods of silver, and gold, of brass, iron, wood, and stone, which see not, nor hear, nor know" (Daniel 5:23)—that is, in idols. This I find to be a dominant theme in the Old Testament. Whatever thing a man sets his heart and his trust in most is his god; and if his god doesn't also happen to be the true and living God of Israel, that man is laboring in idolatry.[22]

I believe now is the time to put Nephi's words to use and liken them unto ourselves:

> Wherefore I spake unto them, saying: Hear ye the words of the prophet, ye who are a remnant of the house of Israel, a branch who have been broken off: hear ye the words of the prophet, which were written unto all the house of Israel, and liken them unto yourselves, that ye may have hope as well as your brethren from whom ye have been broken off; for after this manner has the prophet written. (1 Nephi 19:24)

The Lord has blessed us, the people now residing on this earth, with prosperity unequaled in any other dispensation of time. These abundant blessings have been wonderful in their scope and meaning, but once again man has begun to worship them as false gods. Now these materialistic false gods (idols) have power over those who worship them. Have we been blessed with more of the good things of the earth than our faith can stand?

Much of the population of this planet now spends most of their time working in the service of idols—false gods, which include money, investment portfolios, property, homes, furnishings, vehicles, and other things to gratify their own selves rather than to fill the real and eternal needs of their families or to build up the kingdom of God here on the earth. These blessings are not being used to bless others, the hungry, the needy, the naked, the sick and the afflicted, or to help the missionary efforts and the Lord.

As I study the scriptures, I see more clearly why the commandment, "Thou shalt have no other gods before me" is the first of the Ten Commandments.

In conclusion to this chapter, I would like to reiterate that I truly believe there are no natural reasons for scarcity of anything in the world today. Where there are shortages, they have been created by the greed of man. Today, because of man's greed, "nearly half of the people in the world still live on less than $2 a day, and a fifth survive on $1 a day or less. Most people in Latin America, the Middle East and Central Asia are poorer than they were at the Cold War's close, despite the fast economic integration of the 1990s. Africans live no longer and have no higher incomes than they did 40 years ago."[23]

I have had the opportunity to live and work in many countries, and have seen an abundance of good soil, water, and sunlight—more than enough to feed, clothe, and adequately care for *all* of God's children.

It is true that some parts of the earth have more natural resources than others. Some countries are primarily desert, while others have fertile farmland, and rich supplies of everything. But on this earth there is an overabundance, enough to take care of everyone, enough to provide all the necessities and the good life for all inhabitants of this planet. God is a loving Father that has provided this abundance so all of his children can be well cared for and be healthy and happy. So why is it that millions of God's children are going hungry, and do not have adequate health care or the basic necessities of life? This is happening because of the "plague" of greed, vanity, and pride. (See chapter 11.)

Notes

1. *Webster's Encyclopedic Unabridged Dictionary,* San Diego: Thunder Bay Press, 2001.

2. *Deseret News,* Semi-Weekly, 9 May 1876.

3. Lisa Carricaburu, "High Costs Make Patients Ignore Prescriptions," *Deseret News,* December 2, 2001.

4. Representative Bernie Sanders, (I-VT.) "A Year of Contrasts: Courage, Sacrifice and Corporate Greed," *Common Dreams NewsCenter,* Feb. 25, 2002.

5. "CEO's–Why They're So Unloved," *Business Week online,* April 22, 2002.

6. Representative Bernie Sanders, (I-VT.) "A Year of Contrasts: Courage, Sacrifice and Corporate Greed," *Common Dreams NewsCenter,* Feb. 25, 2002.

7. Ibid.

8. Bruce R. McConkie, *Mormon Doctrine,* 2d ed. (Salt Lake City: Bookcraft, 1978).

9. Harold B. Lee, "Watch! Be Ye Therefore Ready." *Ensign,* Dec. 1971.

10. Ted Wilson and LaVarr Webb, "More Wisdom Needed, Money-wise," *Deseret News*, April 13, 2003.

11. *Webster's Encyclopedic Unabridged Dictionary,* San Diego: Thunder Bay Press, 2001.

12. Karl Ricks Anderson, *Joseph Smith's Kirtland* (Salt Lake City: Deseret Book), 208.

13. Hugh Nibley, *Approaching Zion,* (Salt Lake City and Provo: Deseret Book, Foundation for Ancient Research and Mormon Studies, 1989), 371.

14. Ibid.

15. Matthias Cowley, *The Life of Wilford Woodruff* (Salt Lake City: Bookcraft, 1964), 487–88.

16. Ibid. 517–18.

17. Ben Fulton, "Salt Lake is Scam Central," *Forbes,* February 23, 1999.

18. Heber C. Kimball, *Deseret News,* May 23, 1931.

19. *Webster's Encyclopedic Unabridged Dictionary,* San Diego: Thunder Bay Press, 2001.

20. Ezra Taft Benson, "Obedience to the Lord's Plan," Conference Report, April 1971; *Ensign,* June 1971.

21. Ezra Taft Benson, "For Security—Look Beyond Materialism," *Instructor,* January 1957.

22. Spencer W. Kimball, "The False Gods We Worship," *Ensign,* June 1976.

23. Joseph Kahn, "Despite Aid, Poverty Still Global Scourge," *Deseret News*, March 18, 2002.

5

Legalized Plagues

Some of the most destructive curses in our generation aren't even considered plagues—they are products. I call these "legalized plagues." These plagues kill millions of people each year with much less media attention or fanfare than any war, outbreak, or natural disaster. Yet they are often the most devastating. Silently, they take our wealth, our health, our families, and even our lives. The incredible thing about these plagues is, they are self-induced, self-imposed, and self-inflicted.

Legalized plagues are produced by merchants of greed, misery, and death with no regard for anyone but themselves. Their secret combinations rank right up with the worst the world has ever known. Because the Lord knew that these things were going to happen, he warned and forewarned us:

> Behold, verily, thus saith the Lord unto you: In consequence of evils and designs which do and will exist in the hearts of conspiring men in the last days, I have warned you, and forewarn you, by giving unto you this word of wisdom by revelation. (D&C 89:4)

The Plague of Tobacco

> And again, tobacco is not for the body, neither for the belly, and is not good for man, but is an herb for bruises and all sick cattle, to be used with judgment and skill. (D&C 89:8).

I have probably been one of the most outspoken people in the Church on the evils of tobacco as I have witnessed firsthand the suffering and pain this plague has brought upon God's children. I have watched with horror as a people that I especially love, the Eastern Europeans, have steadily had their life expectancy reduced because of this modern-day plague. All of God's children are my brothers and sisters. I have been to many hospitals and in the homes of members and non-members all over the former Soviet Union and in the United States who are suffering and dying because of the plague of tobacco. Now I must speak up.

When I started working in the former Soviet Union in the early nineties, the life expectancy of a male was sixty-one years of age. In 1998, when I was called to be the mission president of the Russia Samara Mission, their life expectancy had fallen to fifty-nine years of age. When we left Russia in 2001, the life expectancy of a male was only fifty-seven years. Tobacco is evil; it is disseminated by Satan to bring about both earthly and eternal misery and suffering of mankind.

Tobacco is bringing about earthly degradation in ways the entire world is aware of, but the eternal consequences are even more concerning. Tobacco is one of the most addictive substances on the face of this earth.

Of the world's population of six billion, there are presently approximately 1.4 billion smokers—in other words, one out of every five people on the earth is now a smoker. Health specialists have warned that within the next twenty-one years, tobacco-induced illness is expected to overtake infectious disease as the leading threat to human health worldwide.[1]

It has been estimated that 50 percent of them will die prematurely from tobacco-related illnesses. The average loss of life expectancy for smokers who begin in their teens is from twenty to twenty-five years.[2]

The World Health Organization estimates that based on current trends, the death toll from smoking will rise to ten million people per year by the year 2025. Currently two million deaths occur each year in developed countries and one million in developing countries. By 2025 this proportion will be three million deaths each year in developed countries and seven million deaths per year in lesser-developed countries. *If this is not a plague, then what is?* [3]

Derek Yach, project manager of the World Health Organization's Tobacco Free Initiative, speaking at the World Summit Against Cancer, said, "The world community (should) focus its attention not only on infectious diseases but to address what is going to be the biggest epidemic we have seen of our time–the coming epidemic of cancer and other non communicable diseases."[4]

David Khayat, also speaking at the World Summit Against Cancer stated, "This year cancer will affect 10 million more people, and five or six million people will die from it. For several years, cancer has not had the attention it deserves, given the amount of suffering, despair, fear and worry it causes."[5]

The World Health Organization (WHO) said all tobacco products contain substantial amounts of nicotine, which is absorbed readily from tobacco smoke in the lungs and from smokeless tobacco in the mouth or nose. Nicotine has been clearly recognized as a drug of addiction, and tobacco dependence has been classified as a mental and behavioral disorder according to the WHO International Classification of Diseases, ICD-10 (Classification F17.2). WHO predicts that by the year 2020 there will be twenty million new cancer patients each year.[6]

The Third Global Conference for Cancer organizations was held June 24–27, 2001. Key-note speaker, Dr John R. Seffrin, President Elect of the International Union Against Cancer (UICC), stated, "Tobacco use, and its health and economic consequences, has become a global epidemic. No other illness—including the Black Plague, Smallpox, and AIDS—has killed as many people as tobacco use." Dr. Seffrin presented the following statistics:

> Worldwide, during the previous decade, tobacco use killed more than 30 million people. Currently 3 million people die every year from tobacco related diseases. In other words, tobacco kills about one person every ten seconds.
>
> In the world's middle and low income nations, deaths caused by tobacco use are increasing rapidly, even though the patterns of tobacco-caused death may differ in these nations, (in China, for example, tobacco-caused cancer and lung diseases currently account for substantially more deaths than tobacco-caused heart disease), those increases will at first mirror, and then rapidly surpass the tobacco death toll in the high-income nations.
>
> In the majority of the world's high-income nations, tobacco use is the main cause of preventable death, primarily from cancers, heart and atherosclerotic disease, and chronic obstructive lung diseases.
>
> In all the nations of the world, nearly 1 in 10 people or more than 500 million human beings who are now alive, will die from a tobacco-caused disease. By 2030, or sooner, the World Health Organization estimates that this proportion will rise to 1 in 6 people,

making tobacco use the greatest single cause of death in the world.[7]

If anything else posed a threat of this magnitude to human life, whether disease, war, genocide, natural disaster or any other catastrophe, we would demand immediate international action. For more than thirty years, the Surgeon General has circulated annual reports on the tobacco industry's ongoing efforts to enslave, harm, maim, and kill their prey. In addition, this report shows how the industry schemes to entice children of all nations and people from the developing nations to become victims of their deadly crime against humanity. Nevertheless, worldwide tobacco consumption is the highest it has ever been and is growing daily. Even in the United States, statistics reveal that more people are smoking than they have in years.[8]

The next question is why is the news media so silent when it comes to this global epidemic? I repeat: No other illness, including the Black Plague, smallpox, or AIDS, has killed as many people as tobacco use. I would think this is very newsworthy. So why the silence?

Money talks. Newspapers and magazines obtain a great deal of their income from tobacco advertising. This guarantees silence about the dangers of smoking and other forms of tobacco use.

President Hinckley observed:

> One appreciates the incomparable wisdom of the Lord, who in 1833 in a rural town on the frontier of America spoke these simple and encompassing words. "Tobacco is not good for man." He did not say that one would get lung cancer, or develop heart or respiratory problems if he smoked. He did not produce mountainous statistics or recite case histories. He simply declared that "tobacco is not good for man." That declaration was given as "a principle with promise," (v. 3). It was given as a warning and a forewarning, in consequence of evil and designs which do and will exist in the hearts of conspiring men in the last days, (v. 4). How aptly descriptive these words are in light of what we today observe. Can there be any doubt that it is a Word of Wisdom when great forces, with millions of dollars at their command and some of the cleverest minds in the art of advertising, promote that which sober men of science also now say, is not good for man.[9]

As members of the Church, we have truly been blessed to have been given the Word of Wisdom and to have prophets who regularly update us with knowledge, wisdom, and understanding regarding the harmful effects of substances that enslave and endanger the lives of their users. The gospel is not a philosophy of repression; rather, it is a map providing direction to behavior that provides freedom from enslavement, happiness, and health.

Following is an example of what I am talking about, as President Joseph Fielding Smith provided some very sound updated revelation and advice:

> We have inducements, enticing features come before us through the press, by television particularly, and in other ways to lead our people and all other people astray and away from keeping the commandments of God. I want to raise a warning voice to the members of the Church, and especially to the youth of the Church. Do not pay heed to the wicked and malicious advertising of tobacco nor of liquor. The advertising of tobacco today is one of the greatest offenses and crimes before our Father in Heaven, and those who are guilty of it will one day have to pay the price. They do it now because of greed, but we must not listen to these enticings and to the wicked advertising of things that are detrimental to the body and condemned by our Father in heaven and his Son Jesus Christ, contrary to the gospel they have given to us.[10]

How do tobacco companies make themselves look legitimate in the eyes of the general public while they are killing their customers?

In 1996 alone, the Phillip Morris Company had annual revenues of $55 billion. This exceeds the gross domestic product of many nations—including Ecuador, Guatemala, Kenya, Kuwait, Malaysia and Peru—and is roughly the equivalent of Ireland's and Singapore's.[11]

Tobacco companies now own some of the largest food companies in the world. Following are a few examples: Philip Morris—Kraft, General Foods, Miller Beer, and so on; RJ Reynolds—Nabisco, Del Monte, and so on. In addition, tobacco companies are rapidly purchasing large-scale "legitimate" manufacturing businesses.

The large businesses owned by the tobacco companies purchase products from other large companies. This has become very lucrative for companies doing business with the massive tobacco companies. Therefore, they are drawn in, in order to get their share of the big bucks.

> And there are also secret combinations, even as in times of old, according to the combinations of the devil, for he is the founder of all these things; yea, the founder of murder, and works of darkness; yea,

> and he leadeth them by the neck with a flaxen cord, until he bindeth them with his strong cords forever. (2 Nephi 26:22)

The tobacco companies' secret combinations have bought their way into America politically, socially, and economically. They have made a great many people of this nation and the world dependent on them and have thus created a "legal" right to maim and kill without fear of prosecution—thus creating the largest plague the world has ever known.

> For it cometh to pass that whoso buildeth it up seeketh to overthrow the freedom of all lands, nations, and countries; and it bringeth to pass the destruction of all people, for it is built up by the devil, who is the father of all lies; even that same liar who beguiled our first parents, yea, even that same liar who hath caused man to commit murder from the beginning; who hath hardened the hearts of men that they have murdered the prophets, and stoned them, and cast them out from the beginning. (Ether 8:25)

> And again, I say unto you that the enemy in the secret chambers seeketh your lives. Ye hear of wars in far countries, and you say that there will soon be great wars in far countries, but ye know not the hearts of men in your own land. (D&C 38:28–29)

So What Can We do?

Our security lies in living the laws of God. The Word of Wisdom should be considered a commandment—not just a suggestion—about how to stay healthy:

> Behold, verily, thus saith the Lord unto you: In consequence of evils and designs which do and will exist in the hearts of conspiring men in the last days, I have warned you, and forewarned you, by giving unto you this word of wisdom by revelation. (D&C 89:4)

We know that the Lord gives us commandments because he loves us. Therefore he gives us laws, rules, and commandments to bless us. If we live them, we are immediately and eternally blessed. I especially like the promise found in Doctrine and Covenants:

> And all saints who remember to keep and do these sayings, walking in obedience to the commandments, shall receive health in their navel and marrow to their bones; And shall find wisdom and great

> treasures of knowledge, even hidden treasures; And shall run and not be weary, and shall walk and not faint. And I, the Lord, give unto them a promise, that the destroying angel shall pass by them, as the children of Israel, and not slay them. Amen. (D&C 89:18–21)

A good example of updated modern-day prophecy on the Word of Wisdom is when President J. Reuben Clark Jr. warned us that the Word of Wisdom is a law of the Lord:

> The Word of Wisdom is not a rule of conduct; it is a law–the Lord's law–of health. It was promulgated by Him. The law existed before He told it to us; it would exist if the revelation were blotted out from the book. The Church authorities have nothing to do with the law. God, speaking through the forces of the physical world, has prescribed it, and so long as those forces exist, the law will remain. It is therefore the foolish ignorance of a child to assume that the First Presidency can issue a rule that will permit the use of any of these injurious things without their harmful effects. It would be an easy and, in one sense, a pleasing gesture, as satisfying Church members who wish to use these harmful substances, to declare the Word of Wisdom no longer existent. But such a declaration would be no more efficacious than a declaration that the Law of gravitation no longer operates.[12]

Satan and his secret combinations are hard at work to enslave both the body and mind of man. It is their desire to take away our agency by enslaving us to the use of these earthly and eternal poisons. When Satan was cast out of heaven his objective was, and still is, to deceive and blind men and lead them captive at his will. This he does as people hearken to the enticements of Satan's secret combinations. Satan's main attack is still on free agency, as he knows that when he can get men to yield their agency, he has them well on the way to captivity.

In 1983 President Ezra Taft Benson warned:

> "The Lord foresaw the situation of today when motives for money would cause men to conspire to entice others to take noxious substances into their bodies. Advertisements, which promote beer, wine, liquors, coffee, tobacco, and other harmful substances, are examples of what the Lord foresaw. . . . In all love, we give you warning that Satan and his emissaries will strive to entice you to use harmful substances, because they well know if you partake, your spiritual powers will be inhibited and you will be in their evil power. Stay away from those

> places or people, which would influence you to break the commandments of God. Keep the commandments of God and you will have the wisdom to know and discern that which is evil.[13]

As we put our trust in the Lord, live His Commandments, and follow our modern-day prophets we will be blessed with not only health and strength of body, but also obtain greater faith and wisdom and spiritual growth that will help us in all aspects of this life and all eternity.

Stephen L. Richards had the following to say about this topic:

> The Word of Wisdom is spiritual. It is true that it prohibits the use of deleterious substances and makes provision for the health of the body. But the largest measure of good derived from its observance is in increased faith and the development of more spiritual power and wisdom. Likewise, the most regrettable and damaging effects of its infractions are spiritual, also. Injury to the body may be comparatively trivial to the damage to the soul in the destruction of faith and the retardation of spiritual growth.[14]

Our answer is simple:

> And I heard another voice from heaven, saying, Come out of her [Babylon], my people, that ye be not partakers of her sins, and that ye receive not of her plagues. (Revelation 18:4)

> And go ye out from among the wicked, yourselves. Be ye clean that bear the vessels of the Lord. Even so Amen. (D&C 38:42)

Tobacco control and awareness efforts are necessary throughout the world at all levels. Policies and programs at all levels help to solve this problem, and each plays an important part in bringing about a tobacco-aware population. Even if legislation and regulations are not presently feasible at the federal level, it is possible at municipal and state levels to activate strong legislation, which may later prompt the national government to take appropriate action. Many national policies have come about because of local efforts—spanning from grass-roots organizations to committed individuals. The actions that communities can start with include providing protection from environmental tobacco smoke, enforcing restrictions on the sale of tobacco to minors, providing anti-smoking health education programs, and providing anti-smoking materials and centers to help people quit smoking. People at all levels and from all religions are becoming increasingly interested in helping fight this menace. Therefore, this will be most effective if it is a community effort rather than a church program. When national authorities recognize the growing concern of the people, they will eventually provide support for the efforts. For best and quickest results, communities should work with organizations that have global initiatives on tobacco. There are numerous such organizations on the Internet.

But the most rewarding method of making a difference is to simply love our neighbors. I learned firsthand the blessings that can be derived from community involvement in loving our neighbors and helping overcome some of Satan's plagues.

One of the first things I taught our missionaries when we arrived in the Russia Samara Mission in 1998 was that as missionaries they do not have the "right to choose" who they would teach the gospel to and who they would not. I assured them that every living soul on this planet is a son or daughter of our Father in Heaven and that everyone has the right to hear the gospel so they can use their agency and choose for themselves whether they will join the Church. I also taught the missionaries to put the "as if" principle into practice. "People become what you expect them to be. Treat them *as if* they are champions and there is a good chance they will become just that. You get what you expect out of everyone, including yourself. Expect the most out of others and yourself and you will get it" (Natural Law #58; see appendix).

Shortly after that, a companionship in a small town decided to teach "everyone" in their area the gospel. They determined to do this by teaching large group meetings similar to the ones taught in England in the 1800s. They passed out fliers all over the community and taught everyone they could. One of the people who showed up at one of their meetings was a man with very serious smoking and drinking problems. But that is not all; he had spent five and a half years in prison and was released just a short time prior to coming to this meeting. After the meeting he came up to the missionaries and told them that he knew the Church was true and he wanted to be baptized. The missionaries told him that he would have to hear the six discussions, attend church for a period of time, overcome his tobacco and alcohol addictions, and be interviewed before he could be baptized.

The missionaries taught him and worked very hard with him to help him overcome his smoking and drinking problems. Within a few weeks, he was able to quit drinking and eventually, with the prayers and full support of the missionaries, the members, and with the help of the Lord, he was able to completely give up his tobacco dependency.

He faithfully attended church for a number of months and was free of his addictions. He had a firm testimony of the gospel and was now ready for his baptismal interview. It was the happiest day that branch had ever had.

At the baptismal interview it was discovered that he had spent the five and a half years in prison for murder. The district leader who interviewed him cried as he called to tell me the sad news. I told the disheartened district leader that I would interview the man myself. The next day I interviewed the man. I saw a repentant man who wanted more than anything to become a member of the Lord's Church. I told him I would send my findings to the First Presidency and they would have to decide if he could be baptized.

I sent that letter to the First Presidency and within a very short time received a letter from them stating that I needed to watch him for a period of time and that they would get back to me at a later date to see if he was still faithful.

After a number of months—which seemed like an eternity to both this man and me—I received another letter from the First Presidency. They asked me to interview the man again to see if he had remained faithful, was still attending church on a regular basis, and had continued to avoid his former addictions.

When I interviewed the man, I found that he was the most faithful person in the branch. He never missed a single meeting. His testimony was stronger than ever, and his former addictions were history. I wrote back to the First Presidency with my findings. Within a few weeks, I received a letter from them giving permission to baptize this wonderful man. The very next day we held a baptism for him. It was one of the most spiritual baptisms there had ever been in our mission.

This man then started bringing his friends and family into the Church, becoming the most dedicated member missionary I have ever seen.

He met a woman in the branch who had a little boy. After he had been a member for one year, they went to the temple in Sweden and were married the proper way, for all time and eternity.

After returning from the temple, he found a building that the Church could rent on a full-time basis to use for church meetings. Buildings like that are very hard to find anywhere in Russia, but especially in such a small town. We rented it, and the members at last had a place where they could meet every Sunday and any time during the week. Seminary and Institute classes were then possible, as well as all other Church programs, thanks to this worthy brother.

Two months before I left Russia, I had the privilege of setting this brother apart as the first Russian branch president in that branch. Before that time, missionaries had served as branch presidents. He has proven to be one of the most outstanding branch presidents I have seen anyplace in the world.

Just a few weeks before we returned to the US, this wonderful branch president found a piece of land that the Church could purchase to build a chapel. This will be one of a very few chapels in all of Russia. But that is not the end of the story. It goes on and on as this wonderful brother serves the Lord and his fellow man with his whole heart, might, mind, and strength. He went from a state of darkness and unhappiness to a state of joy and light. He will tell you now that he had the power to give up tobacco and other addictions—and he did it through the power and teachings of Jesus Christ.

This demonstrates several important facts:

1. None of us have the right to judge another person.
2. With the help of the Lord, people can overcome addictions.
3. The Lord will make weak things strong, if we put our trust in him.
4. We are all children of our Father in Heaven, and he loves each of us and wants to give us all the blessings he has.
5. The only hope for the world is The Church of Jesus Christ of Latter-day Saints.

The Alcohol Plague

One of the saddest things I have witnessed is alcoholism, a condition where people are enslaved to the addiction of alcohol. Alcoholics are prisoners within their own bodies. Eventually they become totally and helplessly dependent, and finally die a horrible death. And yet alcohol is often depicted as something that everyone uses, something that is chic, popular, and fun. The advertisements never show the real picture: the drunk who has lost his job, his material possessions, his friends, his family, his self-respect, and finally his life. Anyone who says alcohol is fun is lying.

Both tobacco and alcohol are more deadly than any of the illegal drugs, including heroin, cocaine, speed, and so on, because tobacco and alcohol are "legal." The alcohol companies, with their millions of advertising dollars, have been successful in deceiving the public to the point where people accept alcohol as a socially acceptable way to kill, maim, and harm themselves and others. The alcohol "secret combinations" would have us believe that drinking until we are drunk is not to be looked down on or scorned; rather, it is a right.

Alcohol advertising is everywhere: on highway billboards, in newspapers, magazines, and television, even at sporting events. This deceitful advertising is designed to make this deadly poison that causes brain damage, cancer, heart disease, and cirrhosis of the liver (to name only a few of the health problems caused by alcohol) look not only socially acceptable but also glamorous.

Movie stars, movie producers, magazines, newspapers, radio stations, and television stations are all paid huge sums of lucre to glamorize alcohol. In so doing, they all become part of the secret combination that is here to get gain, with no regard for others, no matter how many lives it claims, or how many families are destroyed in the process.

An interesting conference talk was given almost ninety years ago by then Elder David O. McKay on the dangers of alcohol. It is very reassuring to know that the Church has always done everything in its power to warn and educate members and anyone else who will listen about the dangers of alcohol and everything else that causes harm to God's children:

> The American Society for the study of alcoholic beverages and narcotics recently made a report. You will find it in the Senate Document no. 48 issued May 17th, 1909. Their conclusions are these: Alcohol is not safe as a common beverage in any of its present commercial forms, or for ordinary prescriptions: that it is a thief of all the vitality of the tissues; that its promises of strength are mocking lies; its semblance of power is simply nerve center disturbances that end in ultimate weakness and destruction. That the whiskey problem is a greater problem today in this country than the great white plague. The intemperance in the United States today costs this country over one billion, eight hundred and eighty-three million dollars; that today in this Republic there are over three million drinkers who have been taught that alcohol is a

> mild stimulant and a pleasant tonic, and the worst of it is that nearly all these will say they can quit it, each says, "I can leave it alone." The demon is lying to them always, promising them something which it cannot give.[15]

Now it's time to show what alcohol really is—the drug, the poison, the killer.

The Truth about Alcohol

"It's legal, so why make an issue of it? Besides, prohibition didn't work. And it's not a problem in the LDS Church anyway." Alcohol, the American Council for Drug Education observed, is the oldest and most widely used drug in the world. Nearly half of all Americans over the age of twelve are consumers of alcohol. Two-thirds of all American adults drink alcoholic beverages.

The problem is that alcohol is an extremely addictive depressant that affects the entire central nervous system. Consequently, there are an estimated ten to fifteen million alcoholics or problem drinkers in the United States, with more than 100,000 deaths each year attributed to alcohol. Among the nation's alcoholics and problem drinkers are as many as 4.5 million adolescents, and adolescents are disproportionately involved in alcohol-related automobile accidents, the leading cause of death among Americans fifteen to twenty-four years old.[16]

Beer companies would have their victims believe that beer is less harmful than other forms of alcohol, but, in fact, 12 ounces of beer, 5 ounces of wine, and 1.5 ounces of liquor all contain the same amount of alcohol. Therefore they all have an equal effect on the drinker. All forms of alcohol have the same potential for intoxication and addiction. The number of people who died from alcohol related causes soared in the last decade. Alcohol use is involved in:

- One-half of all crimes
- One-half of all murders, accidental deaths, and suicides
- Almost half of all fatal automobile accidents
- One-third of all drowning, boating, and aviation deaths
- Alcohol contributes to 100,000 deaths annually, making it the third-leading cause of preventable mortality in the United States, after tobacco and diet/activity patterns.[17]

- Alcohol is the most widely used psychoactive drug in the United States.[18]
- Nearly 13.8 million Americans have problems with drinking, including 8.1 million people who are alcoholics. Almost three times as many men (9.8 million) as women (3.9 million) are problem drinkers, and prevalence is highest for both sexes in the 18-to-29 year age group.[19]
- Based on victim reports, each year 183,000 rape and sexual assaults involve alcohol use by the offender. There are 197,000 robberies and 661,000 aggravated assaults and nearly 1.7 million simple assaults that all involve alcohol.[20]
- Alcohol adversely affects all human motor skills, muscle functions, reaction time, eyesight, depth perception, and both day and night vision—everything needed to drive a vehicle. Even low amounts of alcohol impair these abilities.

Instead of the media hype of "euphoria" and "acceptance," it's time to show the real effects of alcohol use:

Foul breath
Depression of judgment
Irritability
Loss of physical coordination
Loss of balance
Unsteady gait
Slurred and/or incoherent speech
Inappropriate or violent behavior
Loss of consciousness
Slowed thinking
Depression
Impaired short-term memory
Blackouts

We need to go one step beyond the smiling drinkers shown in advertisements having a wonderful time to the long-term effects: changes in moods that swing from high to low from euphoria to self-pity, which often leads to aggressiveness and cruelty. A powerful deterrent to the "drinking is wonderful" ads would be to show someone suffering from alcohol withdrawal:

- Tremors
- Agitation
- Anxiety and panic attacks
- Paranoia and delusions
- Hallucinations, usually visual
- Nausea and vomiting
- Increased body temperature
- Elevated blood pressure and heart rate
- Convulsions
- Seizures

Does This Sound like Fun to You?

Richard P. Lindsay observed:

> Cigarette advertising is barred from television while alcohol consumption is permitted to be cleverly depicted in TV commercials as integral to good fellowship and joyous events. To the extent that the alcohol industry is under public attack for what it is selling, it responds with odes to moderation. But these actually are relatively infrequent, since the plague of alcoholism and alcohol consumption is widely accepted as a given in modern life. The alcohol beverage industry spends billions of dollars every year promoting its product, implying benefits such as sophistication, sexiness, peer acceptance and fitness. Advertising is almost pervasive enough to make people forget alcohol is a drug that causes 100,000 deaths every year.[21]

The secret combinations of alcohol have glamorized their deadly poison and have motivated others with lucre to make it appear socially acceptable, elegant, physically attractive, and connected to desirable outcomes such as success, relaxation, romance, and adventure. Yet the truth remains that alcohol is one of the deadliest killers the world has ever known. Alcohol strikes unexpectedly, and the venom works its way throughout the body, reducing the mind, body, and soul first to rubbish, then to death.

One hundred thousand deaths result each year from this deadly poison. This is more than a statistic. This does not include the number of babies that are born each year with fetal alcohol syndrome. This does not include the number of lives and homes ruined because of spousal abuse each year. This figure does not include the number of crimes committed by people using alcohol. This does not include the number of victims of these crimes.

One of the saddest effects of alcohol is the effect of alcohol on unborn babies. Alcohol increases the chances of low birth weight babies and intra-uterine growth retardation, increasing the dangers of infection, feeding difficulties, and long-term developmental problems such as fetal alcohol syndrome. The alcohol consumed by the mother passes through the placenta into the baby's bloodstream and then to the immature liver of the baby, which cannot effectively process this poison. Alcohol depresses the baby's central nervous system and stays in the baby's body for a prolonged time, even after being born. The child then remains intoxicated, suffering withdrawal symptoms long after the alcohol is gone.[22]

Many babies with fetal alcohol syndrome have irreversible physical and or mental abnormalities, including small skulls, abnormal facial features, deformed limbs, joints, fingers, faces, heart defects, retarded growth, retarded mental development, and cleft palates.[23] As they grow older, many are hyperactive and have an assortment of learning and perceptual difficulties. As these children become teenagers, they often have additional physical problems, such as ear infections, hearing and vision loss, and dental problems.[24]

Women who drink even very low amounts of alcohol during pregnancy often give birth to babies with subtle alcohol related neurological and behavioral problems.[25]

Anyone who tells you drinking is fun is a liar. Yet we as a society put up with so many people being killed each year because alcohol is "legal" and "accepted."

What did the Lord tell us about alcohol? Because he loves us, he basically said to not touch it with a ten-foot pole:

> Do not drink wine nor strong drink, thou, nor thy sons with thee, when ye go into the tabernacle of the congregation, lest ye die: it shall be a statute for ever throughout your generations. (Leviticus 10:9)

> But they also have erred through wine, and through strong drink are out of the way; the priest and the prophet have erred through strong drink, they are swallowed up of wine, they are out of the way through strong drink; they err in vision, they stumble in judgment. For all

> tables are full of vomit and filthiness, so that there is no place clean. (Isaiah 28:7–8)

> Envyings, murders, drunkenness, revellings, and such like: of the which I tell you before, as I have also told you in time past, that they which do such things shall not inherit the kingdom of God. (Galatians 5:21)

> And be not drunk with wine, wherein is excess; but be filled with the Spirit. (Ephesians 5:18)

> And, again, strong drinks are not for the belly, but for the washing of your bodies. (D&C 89:7)

> Cease drunkenness: and let your words tend to edifying one another. (D&C 136:24)

> Woe unto them that call evil good, and good evil: that put darkness for light, and light for darkness; that put bitter for sweet, and sweet for bitter! . . .
>
> Woe unto them that are mighty to drink wine, and men of strength to mingle strong drink:
>
> Which justify the wicked for reward, and take away the righteousness of the righteous from him! (Isaiah 5:20, 22–23).

I believe The Lord very aptly describes the evil alcohol secret combination that is pouring out plagues on the world today. When someone tells you drinking is fun, don't walk away—RUN!

The Plague of Pornography

The pornography plague is presently polluting the entire earth and enslaving millions of its inhabitants. This plague is the ugliest of all. Again, like the plagues of tobacco and alcohol, the pornography plague was established by Satan and is currently run by his helpers: the "pornographic secret combination."

Unlike the tobacco and alcohol plagues, law does not protect the pornography plague. Yet it flourishes, because when questioned, perpetrators scream censorship and run to lawyers to protect their so-called "rights." Because of the big money behind pornography, and the protection they receive from unscrupulous lawyers, they keep pouring out their deadly filth. This is not at all what our nation's founders had in mind when they established free speech as part of our Constitution.

Pornography generates eight billion dollars a year.[26] Those who gain financially from this despicable sleaze do not care about the individuals, families, communities, and our nations that are being devastated. Their only concern is self-aggrandizement and self-satisfaction.

Pornography is much more than just obscene literature. It is an angel of death.

Pornography is growing like cancer. It has become increasingly difficult to find a decent program to watch on regular television, and cable is much worse. Pornographic movies are shown on cable television on a regular basis, bringing filth right into the subscriber's home, enabling the industry to trap unsuspecting people, especially the youth. According to Henry Boatwright (Chairman of the U.S. Advisory Board for Social Concerns), approximately 70 percent of the pornographic magazines sold end up in the hands of minors. Women Against Pornography estimates that about 1.2 million children are annually exploited in commercial sex (child pornography and prostitution). People kidnap our children daily and abuse them while pictures are being taken. Most of these children are never seen again.[27]

The movie industry has become more and more evil. The majority of movies today are obscene, lewd, filthy and not fit for human consumption. Such movies are truly a deadly plague that puts the viewer in the devil's territory.

The so-called "adult" books, magazines, and videos that are sold in sleazy porn shops were created by the industry to cause people to lust. Pornography leads viewers of this evil wickedness to commit adultery first in their minds, then in their hearts, and eventually in actuality. Pornography truly was designed by Satan to lead the viewer, step by step, directly down to hell.

> Ye have heard that it was said by them of old time, Thou shalt not commit adultery:
>
> But I say unto you, That whosoever looketh on a woman to lust after her hath committed adultery with her already in his heart. . . .
>
> And if thy right hand offend thee, cut it off, and cast it from thee: for it is profitable for thee that one of thy members should perish, and not that thy whole body should be cast into hell. (Matthew 5:27–28, 30).

The very worst pornographic plague that has beset the entire globe is "cyber porn." The Internet can place the most evil hard-core filth right into the homes of anyone with a computer and an Internet connection. The most terrible and evil pictures, movies, online chat groups, live sex, and virtually every illegal explicit image can be found on web pages and in news groups. The sad part of this plague is it is extremely easy for anyone of any age to view this evil and addictive filth. Often the Internet users of porn are then led to Dial-a-Porn phone calls where the listener hears live pornography on the phone. All this leads to terrible consequences.

President Hinckley could not have been more emphatic when he said:

> We live in a world that is filled with filth and sleaze, a world that reeks of evil. It is all around us. It is on the television screen. It is at the movies. It is in the popular literature. It is on the Internet. You can't afford to watch it, my dear friends. You cannot afford to let that filthy poison touch you. Stay away from it. Avoid it. You can't rent videos and watch them as they portray degrading things. You young men who hold the priesthood of God cannot mix this filth with the holy priesthood. . . . Keep yourselves clean from the dark and disappointing evil of sexual transgression. Walk in the sunlight of that peace which comes from obedience to the commandments of the Lord. . . . Where there is true repentance, there will be forgiveness. That process begins with prayer. The Lord has said, 'He who has repented of his sins, the same is forgiven.[28]

To stay clear of these terrible consequences, we must listen to the Lord and follow His counsel. "Flee fornication. Every sin that a man doeth is without the body; but he that committeth fornication sinneth against his own body" (1 Corinthians 6:18).

In Philippians we are further exhorted:

> Finally, brethren, whatsoever things are true, whatsoever things are honest, whatsoever things are just, whatsoever things are pure, whatsoever things are lovely, whatsoever things are of good report; if there be any virtue, and if there be any praise, think on these things. (Philippians 4:8)

President Hinckley pleaded:

> I fear this may be going on in some of your homes. It is vicious.

> It is lewd and filthy. It is enticing and habit-forming. It will take a young man or woman down to destruction as surely as anything in this world. It is foul sleaze that makes its exploiters wealthy, its victims impoverished. . . . I plead with you to get it out of your life. Get away from it. Stay away from it. Otherwise it will become an obsession. It will destroy your home life. It will destroy your marriage. It will take the good and beautiful out of your relationships and replace them with ugliness and suspicion. To you young men, and to the young women who are your associates, I plead with you not to befoul your minds with this ugly and vicious stuff. It is designed to titillate you, to absorb you into its net. It will take the beautiful out of your life. It will lead you into the dark and ugly.[29]

President Ezra Taft Benson made the following statement in a student leadership conference in Sun Valley Idaho:

> When I think of the increases of sex-sin and I have had the opportunity to look into this question of obscene literature, and the relationship between filthy literature and sex crime—when I look into it, I can't help but believe that in this respect this nation is becoming more sinful rather than less sinful. I can't help but be convinced that Satan is using this powerful tool, this God-given impulse in men and women, to try and destroy God's children. It is very, very real, and it is almost rampant. You find it almost everywhere, at times even among people whom you have looked upon as respectable. Satan recognizes that this is one of his most powerful tools. He tries to promote it, to promulgate it. He tries to sell immodesty. And usually, he starts with immodesty. He tries to emphasize that the body, this physical body, is a beautiful thing; therefore, it should be admired and appreciated. And then the next step is to persuade us that it is to be handled. It is a terrible thing, the evils that are coming from this emphasis upon sex. Sex was created and established by our Heavenly Father for sacred, holy, and high purposes.[30]

What We Can Do

What must we as citizens of this world do to protect ourselves and our families from this terrible plague? First, we must make the right choices ourselves and teach by example. Then we must help our families to make the right choices also. "And if it seem evil unto you to serve the Lord, *choose you this day whom ye will serve;* whether the gods which your fathers served that were on the other side of the flood, or the gods of the

Amorites, in whose land ye dwell: *but as for me and my house, we will serve the Lord*" (Joshua 24:15; emphasis added). "For thus saith the scripture; Choose ye this day, whom ye will serve" (Alma 30:8).

The proclamation from the First Presidency and the Quorum of the Twelve, titled "The Family," states,

> The family is ordained of God. Marriage between a man and a woman is essential to His eternal plan. Children are entitled to birth within the bounds of matrimony, and to be reared by a father and mother who honor marital vows with complete fidelity. Happiness in family life is most likely to be achieved when founded upon the teachings of the Lord Jesus Christ.
>
> We warn that individuals who violate covenants of chastity, who abuse spouse or offspring, or who fail to fulfill family responsibilities will one day stand accountable before God. Further, we warn that the disintegration of the family will bring upon individuals, communities and nations the calamities foretold by ancient and modern prophets.
>
> We call upon responsible citizens and officers of government everywhere to promote these measures designed to maintain and strengthen the family as the fundamental unit of society.[31]

We must understand that Satan will do whatever he can to infiltrate the home; therefore, we must do all we can to offset the attack. This will be best accomplished by teaching the laws and commandments of God with love and pure knowledge. In other words, we must teach correct principles and then allow others to govern themselves. We must also act in a proactive manner to make sure this filth does not enter our homes or minds of our family members. We must make sure that everyone agrees that inappropriate magazines, music, movies, and so on, are simply not acceptable for our family. Then we must "act" to prevent it from entering. We must determine that the Internet server we subscribe to does not provide pornography. Even then it can creep in, so we must obstruct it with software designed for this purpose. There are some very good programs that will block pornography on the Internet and detect inappropriate phrases. A combination of these three components: filtering software, a good Internet provider, and solid family rules for computer use can do much to prevent these influences from entering your family.

President Ezra Taft Benson warned us: "Never have the forces of evil been so insidious, widespread, and enticing. Everywhere there seems to be a cheapening, weakening, downgrading of all that is fine, good, and uplifting – all aimed at our youth, while many of their parents are lulled away into a false security as they enjoy their comfortable complacency."[32]

Next, we must stand up and be counted—being not afraid of the face of man. The Lord was very specific in his instructions:

> Hearken unto me, ye that know righteousness, the people in whose heart is my law; fear ye not the reproach of men, neither be ye afraid of their revilings. (Isaiah 51:7)

And again,

> But with some I am not well pleased, for they will not open their mouths, but they hide the talent which I have given unto them, because of the fear of man. Wo unto such, for mine anger is kindled against them. (D&C 60:2)

President Hinckley closed his remarks about pornography with the following warning:

> I encourage you, my dear friends, to speak up for moral standards in a world where filth, sleaze, pornography, and their whole evil brood are sweeping over us as a flood. In the first place, none of us can afford to be partakers of this rubbish. Not one of us, neither I nor any one of you, can become involved with such things as sleazy videotapes, suggestive television programs, debasing movies, sensual magazines, so-called 900 numbers, or the kind of filth that evidently can be picked up now on the Internet. Avoid them like the plague, for they are a serious and deadly disease.[33]

Those of us that know right from wrong must open our mouths and use our pens and computers to fight against the forces of evil. We must express out concerns to local, state, and national officials, with letters, petitions, and in person about the filth that is tearing down our communities. We must also show our concern by not patronizing stores, gas stations, Internet providers, or any other business that sells pornography. We must let them know why we are not using them and let others know also. We must also stand up and be counted by voting for men and women of integrity as well.

The Plague of Violence

The last plague I would like to include in this chapter is the plague of violence. Violence is not "legal," but marketing violence through the media is. Violence that is brought into our living rooms on television, videos, electronic games, or movies, is maiming and killing individuals, families, communities, and nations.

Violence throughout the world is at an unprecedented level. The September 11, 2001 disaster is a good example of the violence that reigns in the hearts of evil and conspiring men in the last days. "And lest your heart faint, and ye fear for the rumour that shall be heard in the land; a rumour shall both come one year, and after that in another year shall come a rumour and violence in the land, ruler against ruler" (Jeremiah 51:46).

From now until the Second Coming, we can anticipate threats, coming from multiple sources simultaneously. Instability and violence in numerous countries caused by ethnic and religious separatists can be expected to increase.

This will happen, and indeed, is now happening:

> This know also, that in the last days perilous times shall come.
>
> For men shall be lovers of their own selves, covetous, boasters, proud, blasphemers, disobedient to parents, unthankful, unholy,
>
> Without natural affection, trucebreakers, false accusers, incontinent, fierce, despisers of those that are good,
>
> Traitors, heady, highminded, lovers of pleasures more than lovers of God;
>
> Having a form of godliness; but denying the power thereof: from such turn away. (2 Timothy 3:1–5).

Violence has become part of our daily lives because pride, greed, and haughtiness have taken over the hearts and minds of men in positions of power. And these things continue to reap what they have since the beginning of time. "Pride goeth before destruction, and an haughty spirit before a fall" (Proverbs 16:18). "Before destruction the heart of man is haughty, and before honour is humility" (Proverbs 18:12).

But violence not only reigns in the hearts of those in positions of power, it has become an extremely dangerous phenomena throughout the world. Within the past two decades there has been an unprecedented increase in violence among today's youth. Behavioral scientists have concluded in more than 1000 reports that one of the main reasons for this is the so-called "entertainment" they absorb every day, particularly through the influence that television has on them.[34]

The correlation between violence on film and that on our streets and homes is irrefutable. American children spend more time each week watching television than any other activity other than sleeping.[35] The youth of today are saturated in violence. And violence is not limited to television, it is found in rented and purchased videos, music, video games, books, radio, newspapers, comic books, magazines, and unfortunately, even in the real world.

The media glorifies violence to such an extent that it sends a message that violence is an appropriate way to act. When questioned about this flood of violence that is dumped into our living rooms, media producers argue that they are forced by viewers to include extraordinary violence to keep their audience interested. As a result, children get the feeling that the world is more dangerous and violent than it actually is. Exposing children to violence makes them less sensitive to the suffering and problems of others, more fearful of the world and conditions around them, and more apt to act aggressively.

It appears we are living in the time that Moroni referred to when he recorded, "Behold, I speak unto you as if ye were present, and yet ye are not. But behold, Jesus Christ hath shown you unto me, and I know your doing" (Mormon 8:35).

These are "the beginning of sorrows" as the Savior foretold. Many now find their lives burdened with frustration, disappointment, and sorrow. Countless numbers feel helpless in dealing with the chaos that seems to prevail in the world. Many grieve over family members whose values are weakening and whose moral standards are declining. More and more of God's children are suffering as society drifts further and further away from the Lord's commandments.

Joseph B. Wirthlin stated:

> If we are to be on the Lord's side, we must be very careful of the entertainment media we allow into our homes. Parents sometimes allow their children to see and hear things that are objectionable because they have difficulty finding a movie, videotape, or television program that does not contain offensive elements. Rather than ban such entertainment, many parents permit their children to watch a movie with violence or profanity or sexual content, hoping their children will realize that Hollywood's standards do not reflect those of the parents.
>
> Being on the Lords side means not only that we shun evil but also that we seek and cultivate good wherever it can be found, whether within or outside of Church.[36]

All of us, including children, adolescents and adults, are exposed to more media depictions of violence than ever before. Commercial television for children is now more violent than prime-time programs for adults, as many cartoons average more than 80 violent acts per program. Since the introduction of videocassette sales and rentals, pay-per-view TV, cable TV, videogames, and online interactive media, many more children and adolescents have greater access to media with violent content than had ever been available in previous decades. These depictions of violence desensitize children to the effects of violence, increase aggression, and foster a climate of fear.

Without strong action against the ever increasing levels of violent entertainment to which our children are exposed, the levels of violence already connected to this age group—in terms of both victims and offenders, can only be expected to increase.

The sure way to determine if a program is worth watching or not is to ask yourself this question and then honestly answer it and follow the Spirit: Would I watch this program or let my family watch this program if Jesus Christ were sitting in the room with us?

It will take courage to take a stand. But consider the options if we don't. We must look at both the present and eternal consequences.

Statistics from hundreds of studies have all shown the same thing: namely that violence has a very serious impact on children.[37] "Every day 14 American children under the age of 20 are killed and many more are wounded by guns. Approximately 3 million cases of child abuse or neglect are reported in the United States annually. By the age of 18, young people will have viewed an estimated 200,000 acts of violence on T.V."[38]

American children are being exposed to violence on television, movies, video games and music on a daily basis. The media glamorize guns and teaches kids that it is not only okay to resort to violence to solve problems, but even that it is the most effective way to do so.

The secret combinations that produce and distribute media depictions of violence state that they are simply "giving the public what it wants." This is not true, but it is what Satan wants us to have, as he knows the effect it has on the minds of the viewing public.

Fortunately, media violence can be turned off. As parents, it is our responsibility to determine first what is appropriate for our family to watch, read, listen to, and so on, and then establish standards that every member of the family will adhere to. Parents must limit media viewing.

Time spent on television and video games is time that should be spent on more productive activities. Parents need to spend more of their own time reading, studying, and playing with their children. Parents must now take their parental responsibilities even more seriously than in the past and take even better care of their most important responsibility: "And verily I say unto thee that thou shalt lay aside the things of this world, and seek for the things of a better" (D&C 25:10).

Both parents and children need to be diligent and cautious in choosing what types of entertainment are allowed in their homes. Now is the time to determine whom we will serve, for "this life is the time for men to prepare to meet God" (Alma 34:32).

In determining standards for your family, critically ask the following questions about each program watched: What values are being taught? Does this program make violence or illicit sex appear exciting, humorous, or macho? Do the protagonists solve problems without violence? Does this program show how victims of violence suffer? Does this program teach skills or present valuable information? Does watching this program help make me a better person, or is it just a waste of time? Does it lift and inspire or make me feel numb or dull? *If it does not have redeeming value, then it is not fit for human consumption.*

Modern technology can help parents monitor what children are watching. There are devices such as the V-chip, which allows you to program the television so it blocks shows that are rated for violence, sex, profanity, or other unsuitable content. In addition, many cable companies offer parents the option of locking out channels they feel are not suitable for their families. However, nothing can take the place of parents teaching by proper example when it comes to influencing children's behavior and habits:

> Enter not into the path of the wicked, and go not in the way of evil men. Avoid it, pass not by it, turn from it, and pass away. (Proverbs 4:14–15)

In conclusion, I would like to say that each of us has one great power. This great power is the greatest power we have, as it is a gift from God. This most choice gift from God is our agency. The gift of agency is the right and power of choice. The power to choose. Each of us are what we are and who we are because of our choices. "You are what you are because that is exactly what you want to be. You can become much more;

yes anything you want to be, if you desire it enough to work for it, have enough faith that it will happen, and then expect it to happen. Then it will happen" (Natural Law # 57; see appendix).

Each of us can choose to leave harmful substances alone and live in the world and not of the world, and have earthly and eternal joy and happiness. Or we can choose the ways of the world and have both earthly and eternal vexation because of these choices.

President Gordon B. Hinckley wisely observed,

> Our challenge is to lift our thoughts above the filth, to discipline our acts into an example of virtue, to control our words so that we speak only that which is uplifting and leads to growth. These are the steps toward personal purity and virtue, the steps we must take in order to lift and invite others to a higher level of living. These steps are achievable for all of us. The course of our lives is seldom determined by great, life-altering decisions. Our direction is more often set by the small, day-to-day choices that chart the track on which we run. This is the substance of our lives—making choices.[39]

The legalized plagues are here. They are deadly, they are real, and they cause both earthly and eternal vexation. We can avoid them, but we must take a stand, we must be either hot or cold. We cannot be lukewarm. We must stand in holy places. We must decide now whom we will serve—"but as for me and my house, we will serve the Lord" (Joshua 24:15).

Notes

1. Neil Francey, "The Death Toll from Tobacco—A Crime Against Humanity," (Sydney, Australia, September 1998).

2. Ibid.

3. Ibid.

4. Derek Yach, "World Faces Cancer epidemic" Agence France-Presse, June 2000.

5. Ibid.

6. Neil Francey, "The Death Toll from Tobacco—A Crime Against Humanity," (Sydney, Australia, September 1998).

7. Ibid.

8. Ibid.

9. Gordon B. Hinckley, *Teachings of Gordon B. Hinckley,* "Word of Wisdom" (Salt Lake City: Deseret Book, 1997).

10. Joseph Fielding Smith, in Conference Report, Oct. 1960, 51.

11. Neil Francey, "The Death Toll form Tobacco—A Crime Against Humanity," (Sydney, Australia, September 1998).

12. J. Ruben Clark, *Improvement Era* 36 (November 1933): 806.

13. Ezra Taft Benson, *The Teachings of Ezra Taft Benson* (Salt Lake City: Bookcraft, 1988), 478.

14. Stephen L. Richards, in Conference Report, Apr. 1949, 141.

15. David O. McKay. in Conference Report, Oct. 1913, 106.

16. American Council for Drug Education "Basic Facts About Drugs: Alcohol," 1999.

17. J. Michael McGinnis and William H. Foege, "Actual Causes of Death in the United States," *Journal of the American Medical Association* (Nov. 1993): 2208.

18. "National Institute of Alcohol Abuse and Alcoholism," *Eighth Special Report to US Congress on Alcohol and Health,* Sept. 1993, 129.

19. "National Institute of Alcohol Abuse and Alcoholism," *Alcohol Health and Research World,* 1994, 243, 245.

20. U.S. Department of Justice, Alcohol and Crime, "An Analysis of National Data on Prevalence of Alcohol involvement in Crime," Apr. 1998.

21. "LDS Leader Honoured for Fight Against Alcohol Abuse," *LDS Church News,* Oct. 19, 1996.

22. Columbia University College of P&S Complete Home Medical Guide, "Overview of Alcohol-Related Problems," October 2001.

23. American Council for Drug Education, "Basic Facts About Drugs: Alcohol," 1999.

24. Columbia University College of P&S Complete Home Medical Guide, "Overview of Alcohol-Related Problems," October 2001.

25. Ibid.

26. U.S. Department of Justice, "Report of the Attorney General's Task Force on Family Violence," 112.

27. Henry Boatwright, "The Documented Effects of Pornography," *The Forerunner,* Nov. 1990.

28. Gordon B. Hinckley, "A Prophet's Council and Prayer for Youth." Ensign, Jan 2001.

29. Gordon B. Hinckley, "Great Shall be the Peace of Thy Children" *Ensign,* Nov. 2000.

30. (The Great Leadership, BYU Student Leadership Conference, Sun Valley, Idaho, September 1959).

31. "The Family, A Proclamation To The World," General Relief Society Meeting, Sep. 23, 1995.

32. *Teachings of Ezra Taft Benson,* 409.

33. Gordon B. Hinckley, "Inspirational Thoughts," *Ensign,* Jul. 1998.

34. Jean Topperman, "What Do Children Learn From Media Violence," *Children's Advocate,* Jan.–Feb. 1997.

35. American Academy of Paediatrics, "Some Things you Should Know About Children and Television," *Newsletter of the Minnesota Association for the Education of Young Children,* Nov.–Dec. 1994.

36. Joseph B. Wirthlin, *Finding Peace in Our Lives* (Salt Lake City: Deseret Book, 1995), 18.

37. Jean Topperman, "What Do Children Learn From Media Violence."

38. "Violence Prevention: solutions before problems," *Child Health Month,* 1994.

39. Gordon B. Hinckley, *Standing for Something* (New York: Times Books, 2000), 41.

6

Wars and Rumors of Wars

> And ye shall hear of wars and rumours of wars: see that ye be not troubled: for all these things must come to pass, but the end is not yet.
>
> For nation shall rise against nation, and kingdom against kingdom: and there shall be famines, and pestilences, and earthquakes, in divers places.
>
> All these are the beginning of sorrows. (Matthew 24:6–8)

Throughout the world, every newspaper, radio, and TV news report demonstrates how this prophecy is being fulfilled today. Daily, the media shows numerous wars and rumors of wars and conflicts throughout the world. Fighting, bloodshed, and wars are the beginning. Famines, pestilence, earthquakes, plagues, and all other scourges will follow. And so it will be until Christ comes again:

> And in that day shall be heard of wars and rumors of wars, and the whole earth shall be in commotion, and men's hearts shall fail them, and they shall say that Christ delayeth his coming until the end of the earth.
>
> And the love of men shall wax cold, and iniquity shall abound.
>
> And when the time of the Gentiles is come in, a light shall break forth among them that sit in darkness, and it shall be the fullness of my gospel;
>
> But they receive it not; for they perceive not the light, and they turn their hearts from me because of the precepts of men.
>
> And in that generation shall the times of the Gentiles be fulfilled.
>
> And there shall be men standing in that generation, that shall not

> pass until they shall see an overflowing scourge; for a desolating sickness shall cover the land.
>
> But my disciples shall stand in holy places, and shall not be moved; but among the wicked, men shall lift up their voices and curse God and die.
>
> And there shall be earthquakes also in divers places, and many desolations; yet men will harden their hearts against me, and they will take up the sword, one against another, and they will kill one another. (D&C 45:26–33)

The United Nations Peacekeeping Statistical Data and Charts showed there were thirty-four wars and contemporary conflicts throughout the world in November 2000.[1] The time of wars and rumors of wars has begun. The hour of darkness, wars, plagues, and natural disasters that have been prophesied since the beginning are at our doorstep. The people of the world will greatly suffer and the works of man will be destroyed. We are warned in the Doctrine and Covenants,

> For a desolating scourge shall go forth among the inhabitants of the earth, and shall continue to be poured out from time to time, if they repent not, until the earth is empty, and the inhabitants thereof are consumed away and utterly destroyed by the brightness of my coming. (D&C 5:19)

In 2003, I took twenty-one students to Urumqi, China to teach at a large private school with over four thousand students. Shortly after coming to China, two unexpected things happened that caused all of us to be confined within the walls of the school most of the time we were there. The first was the war with Iraq. Because this region has such a large Moslem population, the school authorities kept us locked up to protect us from any extremist that may hate Americans. Then a disease which none of us, or for that matter anyone else had ever heard of before, started killing people throughout China and Southern Asia. It then started spreading to the rest of the world. There is no known cure for the disease and it has health officials all over the world terrified. The disease is Severe Acute Respiratory Syndrome (SARS). Because of SARS all of us were called home early, as were most other groups and individuals working in China at that time. At this period the disease was killing more than ten people each day in China alone and was spreading to many other countries. One of the most frightening things I have ever experienced was going through Beijing where virtually everyone was wearing face masks in hopes of protecting themselves from the spread of this plague; no one knew who might have the disease. SARS virtually closed down this huge city during the time I was there. I truly feel that SARS is one of the desolating scourges that is prophesied to be poured out in the last days.

And further we read in Doctrine and Covenants,

> And plagues shall go forth, and they shall not be taken from the earth until I have completed my work, which shall be cut short in righteousness. (D&C 84:97)

All this will factor into the terrible warfare, pestilence, and pollution. Food and water supplies will be polluted. Most likely this pollution will come from radioactive fallout, biological contaminates, chemical pollutants and conditions of nature such as earthquakes, droughts, heat waves, and other disasters brought about by man's disobedience to God's commandments. This will cause much of the food and water on this planet to become poisonous. Add to the misery terrible earthquakes and other natural disasters that will level large cities. There will be unbearable conditions for many people of the earth, especially in heavily populated areas. Ezra Taft Benson observed,

> The great destructive force which was to be turned loose on the earth and which the prophets for centuries have been calling the 'abomination of desolation' is vividly described by those who saw it in vision (see Matthew 24:15; Joseph Smith–Matthew 1:12, 32). Ours is the first generation to realize how literally these prophecies can be fulfilled now that God, through science, has unlocked the secret to thermonuclear reaction. In the light of these prophecies, there should be no doubt in the mind of any priesthood holder that the human family is headed for trouble. There are rugged days ahead. It is time for every man who wishes to do his duty to get himself prepared–physically, spiritually, and psychologically–for the task which may come at any time, as suddenly as the whirlwind.[2]

War, Pollutions, and Pestilence

War is the most evil practice on the face of the earth. It is Satan's way of organizing his followers to systematically murder, rob, plunder, and commit every wicked and immoral act that is contrary to the commandments of God. War is of the devil and is the result of pride, greed, and lust.

In Revelation chapter 8, we are warned that there will be terrible wars and desolation before Christ returns. Speaking of the nations that will fight against His people in those days, the Lord said,

> And I will plead against him with pestilence and with blood; and I will rain upon him, and upon his bands, and upon the many people that are with him, an overflowing rain, and great hailstones, fire, and brimstone. (Ezekiel 38: 22)

Much of this destruction and desolation may well come from atomic, biological, or chemical warfare. The pollution caused by this warfare could cause yet unheard of diseases, poisoning, and irradiation. Millions would die immediately, but many more would linger on for a period of time while their minds and bodies would experience the daily growth of cancer cells, tumors, and other disruptions of body tissues and other forms of vexation and misery until they eventually succumb to a miserable death. Phil Brennan, writing about biological warfare painted a frightening picture:

> Mass panic, a death toll that defied comprehension and a nation left almost defenseless are certainties in the aftermath of a bio-terrorist attack on the U.S. In a city of 500,000 residents, such as Washington, D.C.—which has an average of 3,000 hospital beds—facilities would be overwhelmed hours before the Centers for Disease Control could even confirm that a biological emergency existed. There is nothing to stop America's enemies from attacking us with biological weapons. It's far less risky than other methods because of the incubation periods in transmitting diseases, and it's difficult to pinpoint where the pathogens came from once they're released. The U.S. government's own studies found that a well-planned attack could be more devastating than a nuclear attack.[3]

Much of our ecosystem could be devastated. Our natural resources including the air we breathe, the water we drink, the plants we eat and the soil, from which all life is fed, could all receive radioactive, chemical, and biological fallout. Plants that grow on the polluted soil would then absorb this pollution and eventually affect man as we consume the plants directly, or the animal products that come from animals that eat the plants. Clouds can carry radioactive and biological contaminants far and wide. The radioactive and polluted dust from these clouds and the rainwater will expose distant areas to radiation and pollution and further vexation. This will bring sickness, misery, and death to many areas far from the war zones. This is all covered in Revelation Chapter 8: It describes exactly what will happen to the earth, the ecosystem, and the inhabitants thereon, including man and animal life:

> And the angel took the censer, and filled it with fire of the altar, and cast it into the earth: and there were voices, and thunderings, and lightnings, and an earthquake. . . .
>
> The first angel sounded, and there followed hail and fire mingled with blood, and they were cast upon the earth: and the third part of trees was burnt up, and all green grass was burnt up.
>
> And the second angel sounded, and as it were a great mountain burning with fire was cast into the sea: and the third part of the sea became blood:
>
> And the third part of the creatures which were in the sea, and had life, died; and the third part of the ships were destroyed.
>
> And the third angel sounded, and there fell a great star from heaven, burning as it were a lamp, and it fell upon the third part of the rivers, and upon the fountains of waters;
>
> And the name of the star is called Wormwood: and the third part of the waters became wormwood: and many men died of the waters, because they were made bitter.
>
> And the fourth angel sounded, and the third part of the sun was smitten, and the third part of the moon and the third part of the stars; so as the third part of them was darkened, and the day shone not for a third part of it, and the night likewise. (Revelation 8:5, 7–12)

Modern scripture also echoes the judgments of God that will come upon the world shortly after the opening of the seventh seal:

> And also cometh the testimony of the voice of thunderings, and the voice of lightnings, and the voice of tempests, and the voice of the waves of the sea heaving themselves beyond their bounds. And all things shall be in commotion; and surely, men's hearts shall fail them; for fear shall come upon all people. (D&C 88:90–91).

We are unfortunately aware that presently a number of nations are building up large stockpiles of chemical and biological weapons. Biological weapons are created with the intent to kill large numbers of people by spreading bacteria to people or animals that people consume. The world is experiencing the initial effects of this modern way to kill. Tularemia, smallpox, plague (Black Death), anthrax, viral hemorrhagic fever (Ebola and Marburg), cholera, salmonellas, q-fever, and botulism are some of the main ones now. In addition, there are several livestock diseases that are being stored that can kill large numbers of livestock—another factor that can lead to famine for their enemies. If these tools are used, the wars of this era will be unlike anything the world has ever known—a fiendish combination of modern technology and the evil that has taken over the minds and hearts of this generation.

One might ask, "How will this affect those faithful followers of the Lord? Those who live the commandments?" This is why the Second Coming is called the *great* and *dreadful* day of the Lord. For those who are living the commandments, it will be the greatest day that has happened since Christ was on the earth some two thousand years ago. But for the wicked, it will be the most dreadful event since the world began.

Who will see the coming of Christ as a *dreadful* day? "The fearful, and unbelieving, and the abominable, and murderers, and whoremongers, and sorcerers, and idolaters, and all liars, shall have their part in the lake which burneth with fire and brimstone: which is the second death" (Revelation 21:8). Or to make it completely clear:

> Last of all, these all are they who will not be gathered with the saints, to be caught up unto the church of the Firstborn, and received into the cloud.
>
> These are they who are liars, and sorcerers, and adulterers, and whoremongers, and whosoever loves and makes a lie.
>
> These are they who suffer the wrath of God on earth.
>
> These are they who suffer the vengeance of eternal fire.
>
> These are they who are cast down to hell and suffer the wrath of Almighty God, until the fulness of times, when Christ shall have subdued all enemies under his feet, and shall have perfected his work. (D&C 76:102–106)

Who will see this the *great* day of the Lord? "He that overcometh shall inherit all things; and I will be his God, and he shall be my son" (Revelation 21:7). This is the good news of the gospel. The scriptures state time and time again in many ways the rewards for those who live the commandments and they assure us that if we live the commandments we have no need to fear. "Nevertheless, Zion shall escape *if* she observe to do all things whatsoever I have commanded her" (D&C 97:25; emphasis added).

The scriptures also let us know what the fate of those members of the Church who do not live the commandments will be:

> But if she observe not to do whatsoever I have commanded her, I will visit her according to all her works, with sore affliction, with pestilence, with plague, with sword, with vengeance, with devouring fire. (D&C 97:26)

The choice is ours. Each of us must make the final decision:

> Nevertheless, let it be read this once to her ears, that I, the Lord, have accepted of her offering; and if she sin no more none of these things shall come upon her; And I will bless her with blessings, and multiply a multiplicity of blessings upon her, and upon her generations forever and ever, saith the Lord your God. Amen. (D&C 97:27–28)

Speaking to us individually, the Lord has said,

> Nevertheless, he that endureth in faith and doeth my will, the same shall overcome, and shall receive an inheritance upon the earth when the day of transfiguration shall come. (D&C 63:20)

> For verily I say unto you, I will that ye should overcome the world; wherefore I will have compassion upon you. (D&C 64:2)

In other words, the Lord is telling us,

> I, the Lord, am bound when ye do what I say; but when ye do not what I say, ye have no promise. (D&C 82:10)

As we ponder the signs and events concerning the prophecies of the last days, we must remember the instructions the Lord gave to His people living during this time. The Lord told us to carry the gospel to the entire world. He warned us of conditions, which will exist on the earth preceding his Second Coming. Most people of the earth will reject the teachings of the Lord and his commandments and will not listen to the missionaries. False doctrines will arise and there will be wars and rumors of wars because of the evil that reigns in the hearts of men. Nation is rising against nation. Peace is indeed being taken from the earth, but His disciples must remain faithful and true to their covenants to the end.

Fortunately, the Lord in his foreknowledge takes even our most horrible inhumanity to each other and turns it into something positive—and there is one positive thing that is happening because of the wars. The doors of the nations are being opened up to missionary work, as the people are humbled because of the wars and other desolation worldwide. The Lord is opening every door and is making it possible for us to teach the gospel to every nation, kindred, tongue, and people before he comes again. As members of the Church, it is our calling and responsibility to spread the gospel while the rest of the world is at war. We have witnessed God's hand in bringing down Communism in the former Soviet Union, and he will make it possible for his gospel to go to the whole world.

Elder Levi Edgar Young taught that the wars and desolation will ultimately benefit the Church:

> This is a day of sore trial for all the inhabitants of the earth. Nations are tottering and governments are in danger of being overthrown. Hardly a day passes but what we hear of some terrible catastrophe or some awful tribulation that has come to the children of men. Darkness covers the earth, and gross darkness the people. We are being disciplined; and when we come to know the wisdom of this, we will look upon the whole of life as a means of sanctification. . . . I sincerely believe that these days are bringing us closer and closer to God.[4]

In 1960 David O. McKay said: "A new religious freedom must come. God will overrule it [Communism] for that people must hear the truth and truth in simplicity. Truly there is much for the Church to do in the coming century."[5]

Who would have ever predicted that the Berlin wall could come down so quickly or that communism would disappear in the blink of an eye? In one way or another, the Lord will also open the doors to China and the Muslim nations so the people will have the opportunity to hear the gospel before the Second Coming:

> And I saw another angel fly in the midst of heaven, having the everlasting gospel to preach unto them that dwell on the earth, and to every nation, and kindred, and tongue, and people, Saying with a loud voice, Fear God, and give glory to him; for the hour of his judgment is come: and worship him that made heaven, and earth, and the sea, and the fountains of waters. (Revelation 14:6–7)

The Lord expects it. If we are truly his people, we will all do everything we can to help take the gospel to the whole earth during the times of wars and all other natural and man-made tribulation. And where does it all start? The Prophets have told us that it should start with each of us. They have told us: "Every Member a Missionary." "And ye are called to bring to pass the gathering of mine elect: for mine elect hear my voice and harden not their hearts" (D&C 29:7).

Will most of the people of the world recognize the truthfulness of the gospel and accept Jesus Christ, and be baptized? *No!* We know that there will be few, in comparison to the total number of people on the earth, but it is our responsibility to search out and find those who will accept the gospel:

> For strait is the gate, and narrow the way that leadeth unto the exaltation and continuation of the lives, and few there be that find it, because ye receive me not in the world neither do ye know me. (D&C 132:22)

We have the assurance that all those who do not accept Jesus Christ as their Lord and Savior and live His commandments will be cut off from among the people.

It's sad to think about the evil that encircles the people who do not believe and those who choose not to live the commandments. This "proud and stiffnecked generation" includes people of all ages, classes, and ranks in every nation throughout the world. It is frightening to witness government leaders throughout the world ignore the Lord's commandments. It is sad to see how our leaders in the United States have gone so far that they have outlawed prayer in schools, but support the murder of unborn children, sodomy, adultery, and the slaughter of millions of citizens each year with tobacco and alcohol. Some government leaders now promote the legalization of other deadly drugs and many other unholy and unnatural things that are totally against the laws of God, the laws of this nation, the laws of nature, and common sense. Is it any wonder this world is coming to an end?

Notes

1. "War, Peace and Security World Wide Web Server," *Information Resources Center,* Nov. 2000.

2. *The Teachings of Ezra Taft Benson*, 107–108.

3. Phil Brennan, "Bioterrorism Threat to U.S. Is Real & Deadly," NewsMax.com, Oct. 4, 2001.

4. Levi Edgar Young, in Conference Report, Apr. 1933, 121.

5. David O. McKay, *Church News,* May 28, 1960.

7

Chemical and Biological Warfare

Chemical weapons were first used in World War I when Germany released chlorine gas at Ypres, Belgium in 1915. After that, various aerosol vapor gases were used on numerous occasions by both sides. There were many casualties from this new form of warfare. The Germans began by using the method of simply opening canisters of chlorine and letting the wind disseminate the gas. Chlorine killed or maimed its victims by burning the lungs; it also caused panic among soldiers who were totally unprepared for gas warfare. Then the French put phosgene in a projectile. After that this method became the primary method of delivery. Then in 1917 the Germans used mustard and diphenyl chloroarsine together in shells. The mustard penetrates clothing and inflicts very painful burns and destroys the skin, eyes, and lungs.

Chemical weapons are gaseous, liquid, or solid chemicals, which are used to kill, seriously injure, or incapacitate. The Chemical Weapons Convention defined chemical weapons as "both the toxic chemicals and the ammunition and equipment used to disperse them."[1] Toxic chemicals are defined as any chemical that has the capacity to produce detrimental effects that can cause death, temporary loss of performance, or permanent injury to human or animal life.

People all over the world were shocked and horrified by this new and evil way to maim and kill mankind. In 1925, the Geneva Protocol prohibited use of chemical weapons in warfare from that time on. Several nations, including the United States, signed the agreement with reservations. They signed with the condition that they would not be the first to use chemical weapons, but reserved the right to retaliate in kind if chemical weapons were used against them. In 1975, the United States ratified the protocol completely.

After World War I, several nations that signed the 1925 protocol broke the agreement and used chemical weapons against their enemies. Italy used them on Ethiopia while Japan used them on both Manchuria and China.

During World War II, neither the Allies nor the Axis used chemical weapons, yet both sides built up and stockpiled massive supplies. Since World War II, several nations have used chemical weapons in local wars. Most noteworthy was the Iran-Iraq war of 1982–1987. In that war, Iraq used chemical weapons on its own citizens, killing more than five thousand Halabja Kurds in 1988. In 1995 a cult in Japan released sarin nerve gas in Tokyo subways.[2]

Over the years chemical weapons have significantly increased in toxicity. Today chemical agents are designed to attack the victim through the skin as well as the respiratory system. These powerful agents are designed to penetrate leather and other protective clothing. In addition, today's deadly agents can penetrate protective masks and get right into the respiratory system. The latest developments in chemical weapons have made the agent's delivery to their targets very accurate. Wind and other atmospheric conditions have less and less effect. They are becoming more and more accurate—and more lethal.

Thousands of poisonous chemicals exist, but only about seventy different chemicals have been used as chemical weapons in warfare. The main groups of chemical warfare agents include the following: nerve agents, mustard agents, hydrogen cyanide, tear gases, arsines, psychotomimetic agents, toxins, and potential chemical warfare agents.

Accessibility and Threat of Chemical Weapons

Chemicals of mass destruction have the capability of killing thousands of people with each application. The sad and dangerous truth is they are both readily accessible and inexpensive to produce. Information on how to develop these weapons is available all over the world and with a few technical skills, anyone can produce them. Such weapons may soon become the weapons of choice in the hands of rogue nations, third-rate armies, religious cults, and terrorists.

Because of the ease of getting into this country and the difficulty of detecting each and every method of dispensing chemical weapons, I am afraid it will be just a matter of time until some hate-driven fanatical religious cult and its terrorist affiliates find ways to invade the United States and inflict mass destruction and death on the citizens of this country. Terrorists may spray chemicals from an aerosol can, spread them with a small plane, dispel them from the exhaust of a car as it drives through a populated city, or distribute them in hundreds of other ways.

The thousands of Iraqi citizens who were murdered in 1988 under the direction and command of Saddam Hussein, provides a solemn testimony to the world of Iraq's determination to unleash weapons of mass destruction on mankind. Fortunately, the brave men and women from America, England, and Australia who fought for all of us to prevent his evil designs stopped Saddam Hussein in 2003. But how many other nations like North Korea and Pakistan, along with hate groups and individual deranged people like Bin Laden have the same capability?

Another great danger today is the numerous ongoing insurgencies, separatist movements, and civil wars going on throughout the world. The greatest danger would be from the split of government forces where an opposing fanatical religious hate group might gain access to chemical, biological and nuclear weapons and missiles.

Biological Warfare

> And there shall be men standing in that generation, that shall not pass until they shall see an overflowing scourge; for a desolating sickness shall cover the land. But my disciples shall stand in holy places, and shall not be moved; but among the wicked, men shall lift up their voices and curse God and die. (D&C 45:31–32).

The scourges and desolating sickness described in these verses may well be some of those caused by man's messing with nature, and man's disobedience to one of God's Ten Commandments, "Thou shalt not kill" (Exodus 20:13). Man could well be the creator of these diseases and scourges and bring them on himself. Much of this will probably be the result of biological weapons of war.

In 1859 Elder Charles W. Penrose stated in an article for the Millennial Star:

> Through the rejection of this Gospel, which "Shall be preached

> to all the world as a witness" of the coming of Christ, the world will increase in confusion, doubt, and horrible strife. As the upright in heart, the meek of the earth, withdraw from their midst, so will the spirit of God also be withdrawn from them. The darkness upon their minds in relation to eternal things will become blacker, nations will engage in frightful and bloody warfare, the crimes which are now becoming so frequent will be of continual occurrence, the ties that bind together families and kindred will be disregarded and violated, the passions of human nature will be put to the vilest uses, the very elements around will seem to be affected by the national and social convulsions that will agitate the world, and storms, earthquakes, and appalling disasters by sea and land will cause terror and dismay among the people; new diseases will silently cut their ghastly way through the ranks of the wicked; the earth, soaked with gore and defiled with the filthiness of her inhabitants, will begin to withhold her fruits in their season; the waves of the sea will heave themselves beyond their bounds, and all things will be in commotion; and in the midst of all these calamities, the masterminds among nations will be taken away, and fear will take hold of the hearts of all men.[3]

Again this sounds like biological weapons of mass destruction will play a major role in the plagues, new diseases, terror, and destruction that is prophesied for the last days.

Many people from numerous nations have fallen into Satan's trap and are now working very hard to create the most evil and deadly methods of killing large numbers of God's children through biological warfare. Following are some facts that should be understood about this great evil that will help to fulfill the prophecies of desolating sickness and scourges of the last days:

1. Biological weapons are living organisms adapted for military or terrorist use, intended to cause diseases or death in human, animal or plant life.
2. Between ten and seventeen countries have, or are developing biological agents for warfare at this time.
3. The production of biological agents for warfare does not require expensive specialized equipment and technology.
4. Biological agents for warfare are far more deadly and potent than chemical warfare agents.

5. Very small amounts of biological warfare agents can kill large numbers of human and animal life. It has been estimated that a few grams of some viruses could kill millions of people. Developments in genetic engineering are making these agents even more virulent and difficult to combat.
6. Distribution methods include: artillery shells, missiles, aerial bombs, agriculture sprayers, and crop dusters, to name just a few.
7. Most of the equipment as well as the materials used to produce biological agents for warfare can be readily found, as they are intended for legitimate uses. Therefore, it is extremely difficult to stop the production of these substances.
8. The biological agents are made from organisms, which are highly contagious. In addition, their ability to reproduce causes a devastating impact on human, animal, and plant life.
9. Biological weapons are depicted as low visibility, high potency, readily accessible, and easily delivered.

History of Biological Warfare Agents

The use of biological agents to spread disease, incapacitate, kill or maim an enemy is not a new concept. Incidents of using biological warfare go back many centuries. Up until World War l, biological warfare was primarily accomplished in four ways. First, poisoning food or water with infectious substances. Second, soaking weapons in toxic materials such as manure or in the remains of dead decomposing humans and animals before battle. Third, catapulting corpses infected with plague or other highly infectious diseases over city walls into the enemy's territory. Fourth, sending infected clothing, blankets, or so on to the enemy.

Records as far back as 400 B.C. depict armies dipping swords and arrows into blood, manure, and decomposing bodies before battle. Both Greek and Roman literature discuss the practice of contaminating enemy's water supplies with dead animals and human cadavers. In 190 B.C., Hannibal won a naval victory by dumping containers of venomous snakes into an enemy's ship. In the 14th century, invading armies often besieged cities by catapulting bodies of those who had died of plague into the cities of their enemies. This practice was again initiated in the Russia-Sweden war of 1710, when Russia overwhelmed Reval, Estonia, by catapulting numerous plague-infested corpses over the walls. In the United States, during the French and Indian war, British troops donated smallpox infested blankets to the Indians in an attempt to spread the disease.[4]

Biological warfare as we know it today began during World War I, when the Germans developed anthrax, cholera, and wheat fungus as biological weapons of war. German forces are believed to have used them to a limited extent during that war. The use of both biological and chemical weapons during World War I is what prompted the 1925 Geneva Protocol that was ultimately signed by 108 nations. This agreement was the first multilateral agreement to prohibit the use of both chemical and biological agents as weapons of war. The problem with this protocol was that there were no real methods to verify compliance with the agreement.

During World War II, Japan used biological weapons against China and performed human experiments on Chinese prisoners of war. It is estimated that three thousand victims were exposed to plague, anthrax, syphilis, and other biological agents.

During World War II, several nations including the Untied States began researching and started developing biological weapons of war. The United States as well as other Allied nations developed anthrax and botulism toxins and sufficient amounts were kept on hand for retaliation, in case Japan or Germany made a first attack.

The United States continued to research and build its offensive biological weapons program from the 1950s through 1969. In 1970, the US terminated its offensive biological weapons program for microorganisms and toxins. Then in 1972, the United States signed the Biological Weapons Convention agreement, which was ultimately ratified by 143 countries. The convention addressed prohibition, development, production, stockpiling, and destruction of bacteriologic and toxin weapons. The agreement also required members to submit annual information on what each country did on any further research, but no policing or verification provisions were built into this agreement. Verification and policing was not included in the agreement because at that time, during the Cold War, priority was on nuclear arms control. Consequently, in 1973, the United States completely destroyed its stockpile of biological weapons.

Terrorist organizations pose another great threat, as it is so easy to obtain and create biological agents of warfare. There have been numerous accounts of individuals and groups who have released toxic substances on innocent victims since just 1990.

Because of the problems associated with biological agents used for warfare, the United States and many other nations have concluded that the 1972 treaty is not working, as it is all but impossible to enforce. The United States fully supports the treaty, but believes the current protocol is unworkable.

Since the September 11, 2001 disaster, there have been numerous cases of bio-terrorism in the United States. Anthrax terrorism alone has resulted in more than twenty deaths so far. Interestingly, most cases involved postal workers and media people. The victims were exposed to letters contaminated with anthrax as they handled mail. Because of these terrorist acts, more than 32,000 people with possible exposure to these pathogens have received antibiotics to prevent anthrax.

The possibility of biological weapons being used on both civilian and military targets is higher than it has ever been in history. Defense Secretary Donald H. Rumsfeld recently made the following statement.

> The United States could face terrorist surprises vastly more deadly than the Sept. 11 attacks that killed more than 3,000 people. Terrorists who manage to get unconventional weapons and deliver them great distances with ballistic missiles could kill hundreds of thousands of Americans. The real concern at the present time is the nexus between terrorist networks and terrorist states that have weapons of mass destruction. Let there be no doubt, there is that nexus, and it must force people all across this globe to realize that what we're dealing with here is something that is totally different. It poses risks to not thousands of lives but hundreds of thousands of lives, when one thinks of the power and lethality of those weapons.[5]

FBI Director Robert S. Mueller told reporters, "I believe there are 'sleeper cells' of terrorists waiting for word to attack, and thus the nation remains on high alert. Information about possible threats to Americas have emerged from interviews with captured al-Qaida fighters and an enormous cache of documents, videotapes and other materials recovered in Afghanistan and elsewhere have been obtained."[6]

Biological and chemical weapons have been described as "the poor man's atom bomb." They strike fear into the hearts and minds of both civilians and military personnel because of their massive, devastating capabilities, and they are very difficult to detect and defend against.

It appears that terrorists are everything the Lord hates:

> These six things doth the Lord hate: yea, seven are an abomination unto him:
>
> A proud look, a lying tongue, and hands that shed innocent blood,
>
> An heart that deviseth wicked imaginations, feet that be swift in running to mischief.
>
> A false witness that speaketh lies, and he that soweth discord among brethren. (Proverbs 6:16–19).

Biological agents are also a threat. I could go on about many biological agents, such as anthrax, Q fever, salmonellas, racine, mad cow disease, and brucellosis. But I am sure you get the point. Biological agents of warfare are very real and are being stockpiled around the world—and they will be used.

> For I, the Almighty, have laid my hands upon the nations, to scourge them for their wickedness. And plagues shall go forth, and they shall not be taken from the earth until I have completed my work, which shall be cut short in righteousness. (D&C 84:96–97)

The Threats Within

The threats from within could be as serious as ones from without. Since the September 11, 2001 disaster, the news media have been chock full of reports on everything from chemical weapons to anthrax right here in the United States. The FBI and local police units have warned that domestic fringe organizations such as religious fanatics, right wing militants, ethnic hate groups, and even city gangs, have been showing a great deal of interest in both chemical and biological weapons of war. Numerous investigations of people and groups attempting to develop and use such weapons are now under active investigation by the FBI's antiterrorism unit.

This new era of terrorism has changed the entire world. Weapons of mass destruction can and are getting into the hands of hate groups and individuals who have the intent to murder large numbers of people as an end in itself. It may even come to the point where large nations with nuclear power cannot control small nations that have a stockpile of chemical and biological weapons. Especially if they also have a well organized terrorist organization that is ready, willing, and able to use them.

Prophecies about This New Kind of Warfare

In 1946, President J. Ruben Clark, Jr. understood the potential danger of chemical and biological weapons to mankind and the world in general. In the 1946 General Conference, he warned of the evils and dangers of chemical warfare in his "Protest against Savage Methods"

> Thus we in America are now deliberately searching out and developing the most savage, murderous means of exterminating peoples that Satan can plant in our minds. We do it not only shamelessly, but also with a boast. God will not forgive us for this. If we are to avoid extermination, if the world is not to be wiped out, we must find some way to curb the fiendish ingenuity of men who have apparently no fear of God, man, or the devil, and who are willing to plot and plan and invent instrumentalities that will wipe out all the flesh of the earth. And, as one American citizen of one hundred thirty millions, as one in one billion population of the world, I protest with all of the energy I possess against this fiendish activity, and as an American citizen, I call upon our government and its agencies to see that these unholy experimentations are stopped, and that somehow we get into the minds of our war-minded general staff and its satellites, and into the general staffs of all the world, a proper respect for human life. May God give us the strength to stand in these times of stress and trial and crisis. May he give us the wisdom and the inspiration to put hate out of our hearts, a hate that is consuming us. May he give us the power as a people so to bring our influence to bear that men, mankind, may be saved, I humbly pray in the name of Jesus. Amen.[7]

As members of the Lord's church here on the earth, what should we be doing now and during the times of the desolating wars? I believe now is the time we must love one another. This love must start in our hearts and in our homes. We are called at this time to be peacemakers even though we live in a world filled with wars and rumors of wars. We must also "Trust the Lord" and his unfolding purposes even when his purposes are not clear to us at the moment. And so, as we anticipate a continued increase of wars and rumors of wars prior to the Second Coming, culminating in the great battle of Armageddon, we will put our trust in the Lord.

In 1879 Elder Orson Pratt also warned us about the wars of destruction and the changes that would be coming to the people of this earth.

> When that day shall come there shall be wars, not such wars as have come in centuries and years that are past and gone, but a desolating war. When I say desolating, I mean that it will lay these European nations in waste. Cities will be left vacated, without inhabitants. The people will be destroyed by the sword of their own hands. Not only this but many other cities will be burned; for when contending armies are wrought up with terrible anger, without the Spirit of God upon them, when they have not that spirit of humanity that now characterizes many of the wars amongst the nations, when they are left to themselves, there will be no quarter given, no prisoners taken, but a war of destruction, of desolation, of the burning of the cities and villages, until the land is laid desolate. That is another thing that will come before the coming of the Son of Man.[8]

Just one year after the conclusion of World War II, President George Albert Smith prophesied that if the people of this world would not repent, even greater catastrophes would come than were seen in World War II: "I fear that the time is coming . . . unless we can call the people of this world to repent of their ways, the great war that has just passed will be an insignificant thing, as far as calamity is concerned, compared to that which is before us. And we can avoid it; if we will each do our part, it can be prevented."[9]

If we do our part to live the commandments and follow the council of our prophet we will be blessed during these times by knowing that we are doing all that we can do. The calamities and desolating scourges will come, but if we are doing all we can to serve our fellow man and the Lord, we will be on the right side. We will be in the right place at the right time. This will give us at least peace of mind.

Joseph Fielding Smith, mincing no words, came right to the point. "If prophecy is to be fulfilled, there awaits the world a conflict more dreadful than any the world has yet seen."[10]

A strange thing sometimes happens in the Church. Some members have the misconception that because they are members, all will be well for them during all these calamities. It is true that the righteous will ultimately be saved in the kingdom of God, but it must be understood that many of them will also become causalities of the wars, plagues, pestilence, and destruction that will precede Christ's Second Coming. Even the righteous cannot say, "All is well in Zion." Joseph Smith put it as plain as he could when he said: "The saints will not escape all the judgments, whilst the wicked suffer; for all flesh is subject to suffer, and the righteous shall hardly escape; still many of the Saints will escape, for the just shall live by faith; yet many of the righteous shall fall a prey to disease, to pestilence, etc., by reason of the weakness of the flesh and yet be saved in the Kingdom of God."[11]

On this note, President Ezra Taft Benson also came right to the point.

> Too often we bask in our comfortable complacency and rationalize that the ravages of war, economic disaster, famine and earthquake cannot happen here. Those who believe this are either not acquainted with the revelations of the Lord, or they do not believe them. Those who smugly think these calamities will not happen, that they somehow will be set aside because of the righteousness of the Saints, are deceived and will rue the day they harbored such a delusion. The Lord has warned and forewarned us against a day of great tribulation and given us counsel, through His servants, on how we can be prepared for these difficult times. Have we heeded His counsel? Be faithful, my brothers and sisters, to this counsel and you will be blessed–yes, the most blessed people in all the earth.[12]

Now is the time to turn to the Lord. Now is the time to follow our prophets. Now is the time to study the scriptures in depth. Now is the time to make definite decisions about who we will serve. Now is the time to take a firm stand and be vigilant in our stand. Now is the time to love our neighbor as ourselves. Now is the time to be the example the Lord needs in his Church. Now is the time to share our most valuable possession, our knowledge of the gospel with all of God's children. Yes, now is the time to completely turn our lives over to the Lord.

In 1976 President Spencer W. Kimball put everything into proper perspective:

> We are a warlike people, easily distracted from our assignment of preparing for the coming of the Lord. When enemies rise up, we commit vast resources to the fabrication of gods of stone and steel–ships, planes, missiles, and fortifications–and depend on them for protection and deliverance. When threatened, we become anti-enemy instead of pro-kingdom of God; we train a man in the art of war and call him a patriot, thus in the manner of Satan's counterfeit of true patriotism, perverting the Savior's teaching; "Love your enemies, bless

> them that curse you, do good to them that hate you, and pray for them which despitefully use you, and persecute you; That ye may be the children of your Father which is in heaven" (Matthew 5:44-45). What are we to fear when the Lord is with us? Can we not take the Lord at his word and exercise a particle of faith in him? Our assignment is affirmative: to forsake the things of the world as ends in themselves; to leave off idolatry and press forward in faith; to carry the gospel to our enemies, that they might no longer be our enemies.[13]

With an understanding of the devastating effects of biological weapons and the evil that reins on the earth today, we can understand what is described in Matthew 24:

> When ye therefore shall see the abomination of desolation, spoken of by Daniel the prophet, stand in the holy place, (whoso readeth, let him understand:)
>
> Then let them which be in Judaea flee into the mountains.
>
> Let him which is on the housetop not come down to take any thing out of his house:
>
> Neither let him which is in the field return back to take his clothes.
>
> And woe unto them that are with child, and to them that give suck in those days!
>
> But pray ye that your flight be not in the winter, neither on the sabbath day:
>
> For then shall be great tribulation, such as was not since the beginning of the world to this time, no, nor ever shall be.
>
> And except those days should be shortened, there should no flesh be saved: but for the elect's sake those days shall be shortened. (Matthew 24:15–22)

On Christmas day in 1832, Joseph Smith received a revelation on war that revealed what was going to happen on the earth as far as wars from that day until Christ returns. It is interesting to see how much of that prophecy has already taken place and how much is happening today:

> And the time will come that war will be poured out upon all nations, beginning at this place. . . .
>
> And thus, with the sword and by bloodshed the inhabitants of the earth shall mourn; and with famine, and plague, and earthquake, and the thunder of heaven, and the fierce and vivid lightning also, shall the inhabitants of the earth be made to feel the wrath, and indignation, and

> chastening hand of an Almighty God, until the consumption decreed hath made a full end of all nations. . . .
>
> Wherefore, stand ye in holy places, and be not moved, until the day of the Lord come; for behold, it cometh quickly, saith the Lord, Amen. (D&C 87:2, 6, 8)

It is wonderful to know that in the midst of all the terrible destruction that will be poured out, we can and will be blessed if we will simply do four things. (1) Trust in the Lord. (2) Live His commandments. (3) Stand in holy places. (4) Do our part to spread the gospel to every nation kindred and tongue.

> Therefore, verily, thus saith the Lord, let Zion rejoice, for this is Zion—THE PURE IN HEART; therefore, let Zion rejoice, while all the wicked shall mourn.
>
> For behold, and lo, vengeance cometh speedily upon the ungodly as the whirlwind; and who shall escape it?
>
> The Lord's scourge shall pass over by night and by day, and the report thereof shall vex all people; yea, it shall not be stayed until the Lord come;
>
> For the indignation of the Lord is kindled against their abominations and all their wicked works.
>
> Nevertheless, Zion shall escape if she observe to do all things whatsoever I have commanded her.
>
> But if she observe not to do whatsoever I have commanded her, I will visit her according to all her works, with sore affliction, with pestilence, with plague, with sword, with vengeance, with devouring fire. (D&C 97:21–26)

The Lord's Plan Will Be Accomplished

At times it may appear that Satan is succeeding in promoting war and contention, but it is very important to always remember that in the end, it will be the Lord's eternal plan that will be accomplished:

> For have I not the fowls of heaven, and also the fish of the sea, and the beasts of the mountains? Have I not made the earth? Do I not hold the destinies of all the armies of the nations of the earth? (D&C 117:6)

President John Taylor wisely observed: "Whatever the opinions and ideas of men may be, it will be found at last that the Lord rules, manipulates and manages the affairs of men, of nations and of the world, and therefore, neither this nation nor any other nation can do anything more than God permits. He sets up one nation, and puts down another, according to the counsels of his own will. And he has done this from the beginning, whether men believe it or not."[14]

In the April 1959 General Conference, George Q. Morris noted:

> Bear in mind that the Lord is directing this world. We are frequently reminded that conditions have been so developed in the powers of warfare that an accident or a rash move could set in operation those powers which might destroy our civilization. But let us bear in mind that this world is in the hands of God. All these things will happen only so far as they are in accordance with his plans and his purposes. And let us not waste our time and our energy and get into a nervous condition about what is going to happen to the world. That is not our sphere of responsibility. The Lord will take care of that. It remains for us to be devoted to the up-building of his kingdom and facing whatever conditions may come to us.[15]

The wars will rage, the famines will come, pestilence will occur; the plagues will be upon us. But if we put our trust in the Lord, live his commandments, stand in holy places and do all we can to further his work and be true disciples, then let it all come to pass. Who cares? We will be on the right side—the winning side. And in the end, we will receive eternal life in the celestial kingdom to live with God the Father and God the Son forever. If all this is the Lord's plan and it is, and if we are on the right team, we have no need to fear. So let it happen. Bring it on.

What Should Members Do?

As members of the Church, now is the time to put our trust in the Lord and do what he has been telling us to do since the beginning:

> Love your enemies, bless them that curse you, do good to them that hate you, and pray for them which despitefully use you, and persecute you; That ye may be the children of your Father which is in heaven. (Matthew 5:44–45)

We have no need to fear when the Lord is with us. So let's take the Lord at his word and put our trust and faith in him. Our assignment is to press forward in faith and take the gospel to our enemies, so they will no longer be enemies, but our brothers and sisters in the gospel.

Now is the time to put the first two great commandments into practice:

> And thou shalt love the Lord thy God with all thy heart, and with all thy soul, and with all thy mind, and with all thy strength: this is the first commandment. And the second is like, namely this; thou shalt love thy neighbor as thyself. There is none other commandment greater than these. (Mark 12:30–31)

What should we as members of the Church do now that the wars and rumors of war are upon the earth, knowing that death and destruction will continue to increase every year until Christ comes again? What would the Lord have "his people" do during these trying times? I truly believe that if we want peace and safety, we as the Lord's people must prepare for peace—not war. In other words, now is the time to make peace with our God, and our fellow man, and proclaim peace to the entire world. Ezra Taft Benson said this:

> I think that if you are going to be successful, you must develop in your heart a love for people with whom you work. They need the gospel as they need no other thing. Develop in your hearts a love for them, a desire to lift them up, and a desire to help them and to bless them by teaching them the principles of the gospel. The gospel will absolutely revolutionalize their lives and change their outlook. People are hungry for something that will give them an anchor, that will satisfy the questions of their souls that will bring peace to their hearts and a feeling of security, inner satisfaction.[16]

We must live in such a way that the entire world knows there is one people left that they can look to as an example of righteous living. We must teach and encourage peace and the hope of Christ to all mankind. The only way we can truly do this is by living it, so we can teach by example. Then we must do what the Lord expects us to do, namely, to share the gospel with every nation, kindred, and tongue until everyone in the world has had the opportunity to hear the gospel. Then they can make their own decision as to whom they will follow, Christ or Satan, and what they will receive, liberty or death. When we have completed our assignment to take the gospel to the entire world, Christ will return and peace will reign for one thousand years. This is why we must prepare for peace not war.

David O. McKay said, "The greatest need of this world today is peace. The turbulent storms of hate, of enmity, of distrust, and of sin are threatening to wreck humanity. It is time for men—true men—to dedicate their lives to God, and to cry with the spirit and power of Christ, Peace be still!"[17]

We know it is Satan's plan to do everything he and his evil forces can to stop or at least slow down the work of the Lord, especially missionary work. Therefore, we can expect continued and greatly increased opposition to our efforts to further the work of the Lord. We can anticipate a vast expansion of opposition from all areas. In addition, our religious freedoms will be curtailed in many ways throughout the world. We will be criticized more for taking moral stands and living the commandments of the Lord. Social pressure will increase. Other religions might reject us. Governments will abandon us. Our political rights and freedoms might erode. And in general we can expect greater persecution as a people and religion. In other words, Satan will wage war against us because we are on the Lord's side. The wicked and evil forces will combine to trample us under foot, and wage war against the Saints for the purpose of destroying us.

> . . . for we beheld Satan, that old serpent, even the devil, who rebelled against God, and sought to take the kingdom of our God and his Christ—
>
> Wherefore, he maketh war with the saints of God, and encompasseth them round about.
>
> And we saw a vision of the sufferings of those with whom he made war and overcame, for thus came the voice of the Lord unto us. (D&C 76:28–30)

> And again, I will give unto you a pattern in all things, that ye may not be deceived; for Satan is abroad in the land, and he goeth forth deceiving the nations. (D&C 52:14)

What can we do to withstand the coming persecution and endure the evil that will come upon the Lord's people? Now more than ever, we must put our full trust in the Lord. We can no longer do things our way. "Be not wise in thine own eyes: fear the Lord, and depart from evil" (Proverbs 3:7). We must live the commandments. "Let us hear the conclusion of the whole matter: Fear God, and keep his commandments: for this is the whole duty of man" (Ecclesiastes 12:13).

Even though we will be persecuted for doing the will of the Lord, we still must do good to everyone, forgive and forget, learn to turn the other cheek, be humble, and eliminate pride and vanity. Also, we cannot be "respecters of persons," or be "afraid of the face of man." We are to reverence only God.

> And I say unto you my friends, Be not afraid of them that kill the body, and after that have no more that they can do. But I will forewarn you whom ye shall fear: Fear him, which after he hath killed hath power to cast into hell; yea, I say unto you, Fear him. (Luke 12:4–5)

We must maintain and increase our trust and faith in the Lord. He will overcome all; therefore it is our responsibility to understand that all these things are necessary to accomplish the divine mandate of God the Father. Now is the time to choose to be on the Lord's side and to stand in holy places.

God gives everyone agency to choose for themselves. We each have the opportunity to choose to follow the Lord and keep ourselves unspotted from the world, or accept Satan's evil, deceptive, lustful, and worldly counterfeits. Everyone has this agency. Many will choose the path to follow Satan. Some will even become so possessed by evil that they will try to destroy the Saints and Lord's work on the earth. They have their agency to so choose in this life; each of us will demonstrate precisely which side we are on. In the end, each of us will have made the decision. This is how the Lord will justify our reward or fate after this mortal probationary period.

Some members ask, "What if the evil forces, including men, armies, and governments take over and scatter, destroy, maim, and kill us and our families?" Again, I would say, "Put your trust in the Lord." If we are living the Gospel as we should, we have no need to fear, for the Lord is on our side—or I should say we are on the Lord's side:

> For he will give unto the faithful line upon line, precept upon precept; and I will try you and prove you herewith.
>
> And whoso layeth down his life in my cause, for my name's sake, shall find it again, even life eternal.
>
> Therefore, be not afraid of your enemies, for I have decreed in my heart, saith the Lord, that I will prove you in all things, whether you will abide in my covenant, even unto death, that you may be found worthy.

> For if ye will not abide in my covenant ye are not worthy of me.
>
> Therefore, renounce war and proclaim peace, and seek diligently to turn the hearts of the children to their fathers, and the hearts of the fathers to the children. (D&C 98:12–16)

> And again, this is the law that I gave unto mine ancients, that they should not go out unto battle against any nation, kindred, tongue, or people, save I, the Lord, commanded them. (D&C 98:33)

The Lord wants a righteous people. If we are to be his people, and are to be called Saints of the latter days, we must do his will. This includes living his commandments and proclaiming peace and teaching the gospel to every nation, kindred, and tongue. Let's make it happen! When? Now! Who? All of us!

We do not need to worry about the wars and other calamities that are here now and will be increasing. Rather, we can look forward to the coming of the Savior and be glad. The Lord said, "Be not troubled, for, when all these things shall come to pass, ye may know that the promises which have been made unto you shall be fulfilled" (D&C 45:35).

The Lord also said,

> For they that are wise and have received the truth, and have taken the Holy Spirit for their guide, and have not been deceived—verily I say unto you, they shall not be hewn down and cast into the fire, but shall abide the day.
>
> And the earth shall be given unto them for an inheritance; and they shall multiply and wax strong, and their children shall grow up without sin unto salvation.
>
> For the Lord shall be in their midst, and his glory shall be upon them, and he will be their king and their lawgiver. (D&C 45:57–59)

I would like to conclude this chapter with two things. First a quote found in the Doctrine and Covenants, "If ye are prepared ye shall not fear" (D&C 38:30), and then a statement by Elder John A. Widtsoe given in 1942 at the height of World War II:

> Speaking to the Church about the events of the last days, the Lord said, 'The wicked shall flee unto Zion for safety.' Since Zion is wherever the pure in heart are, I like to read into that inspired saying that there is safety wherever the people of the Lord live so worthily as to claim the sacred title of citizens of the Zion of our Lord. Otherwise the name

Zion is but an empty sound. The only safety that we can expect in this or any other calamitous time lies in our conformity to gospel requirements.

In this world of upheaval, in this day of wanton destruction, we, as a people must look upward. There must be trust and faith in our hearts. Hope must walk by our side. We must remember charity also. We must treasure the warm words of the Father to His Church. "Be of good cheer, and do not fear, for I the Lord am with you, and will stand by you" (D&C 68: 6). We who have been called to leadership in the Church of Christ must lead our people from anxiety and fear and doubt, to trust and faith in the Lord, and certainty in the outcome of the Lord's plan of salvation. We must repeat with gladness the words of the Lord, 'Fear not, let your hearts be comforted; yea, rejoice evermore, and in everything give thanks' (D&C 98:1).

It is our destiny as a people to purify the world; to lead men from evil to good; to win the nations to the realm of everlasting truth; to prepare the earth for the coming of the Lord. We are called to establish the kingdom of God on earth. If we accept our mission with faith and the courage born of faith, the Lord will make us victorious in our labors in his cause. Happiness will wait upon us. The protection of heaven will be about us. At this time in our history, let us teach as never before. 'If ye are prepared, ye shall not fear.[18]

Notes

1. "Organization for the Prohibition of Chemical Weapons," *Chemical Warfare Agents,* last modified 29 April 1997 by ICA Division, OPCW.

2. University of Wisconsin, Board of Regents, *Chemical Weapons in History,* 2001.

3. Charles W. Penrose, "Millennial Star," *Journal of Discourses,* 21 (Sept. 19, 1859): 582.

4. Daniel J. Dire, M. D., "Biological Warfare Agents," eMedicine Journal, 3, no. 1 (January 2002).

5. Robert Burns, "Rumsfeld Warns of Threats Deadlier Than Attacks," *Chicago Tribune Internet Edition*, Jan. 2002.

6. Ibid.

7. J. Reuben Clark, Jr., in Conference Report, Oct. 1946.

8. Orson Pratt, *Journal of Discourses,* 18 (1879).

9. George Albert Smith, *The Improvement Era,* Nov. 1946, 763.

10. Joseph Fielding Smith, *Signs of the Times,* 116, 120–21.

11. *History of the Church,* vol. 4, 11.

12. Ezra Taft Benson, in Conference Report, Oct. 1980; *Ensign,* Nov. 1980, 34.

13. Spencer W. Kimball, "The False Gods We Worship," *Ensign,* Jun. 1976. 3.

14. John Taylor, *Journal of Discourses,* vol. 23, 333

15. George Q. Morris, in Conference Report, Apr. 1959, 102

16. Ezra Taft Benson, "Charity and Love," *The Teachings of Ezra Taft Benson,* 276.

17. Spencer W. Kimball, "The Miracle of Forgiveness," (Salt Lake City: Bookcraft, 1969), 363.

18. John A. Widtsoe, in Conference Report, Apr. 1942, 33.

8

Class Warfare

Fourth Nephi describes how after all the Nephites and Lamanites were converted to the Church of Christ, they lived in harmony with each other and all had everything in common. During this time the people were able to work miracles, and everyone prospered in the land.

Because they had all things in common and believed in Christ, they prospered:

> And they had all things common among them; therefore there were not rich and poor, bond and free, but they were all made free, and partakers of the heavenly gift. (4 Nephi 1:3)

During this time they were all extremely blessed by the Lord. "And the Lord did prosper them exceedingly in the land; yea, insomuch that they did build cities again where there had been cities burned" (4 Nephi 1:7).

In essence, everyone was blessed and all prospered because all people were equal. There were no classes or class distinctions. This must have been one of the very best times and places to live on the earth:

> And it came to pass that there was no contention in the land, because of the love of God which did dwell in the hearts of the people. And there were no envying nor strifes, nor tumults, nor whoredoms, nor lyings, nor murders, nor any manner of lasciviousness; and surely there could not be a happier people among all the people who had been created by the hand of God. (4 Nephi 1:15–16)

This was more than Satan could stand, because he wants everyone to be miserable like himself. So Satan and his followers tempted them with pride, because "pride" is his best tool. With pride in their hearts, soon greed took over. Classes and class distinction followed. After that came secret combinations and other sins. This directly led to class warfare, and real warfare followed, which eventually destroyed the entire Nephite nation.

Mormon Describes This to Us:

> And it came to pass that two hundred years had passed away; and the second generation had all passed away save it were a few.
>
> And now I, Mormon, would that ye should know that the people had multiplied, insomuch that they were spread upon all the face of the land, and that they had become exceedingly rich, because of their prosperity in Christ.
>
> And now, in this two hundred and first year there began to be among them those who were lifted up in *pride,* such as the wearing of costly apparel, and all manner of fine pearls, and of the fine things of the world.
>
> And from that time forth they did have their goods and their substance no more common among them.
>
> And they began to be divided into *classes*; and they began to build up churches unto themselves to get gain, and began to deny the true church of Christ. (4 Nephi 1:22–26; emphasis added).

The classes that were first established included the Nephites, Jacobites, Josephites, and Zoraminites, who, for a period, remained believers in Christ. And those who willfully rebelled against the gospel of Christ once again called themselves Lamanites, Lemuelites, and Ishmaleites.

With classes once more in place, it was now time for Satan to bring on the next stage of greed and pride. That was the return of the secret oaths and combinations of Gadianton. Secret combinations rapidly spread over the whole land and eventually engulfed the Nephites as well as the Lamanites, because of their pride and love of riches.

Eventually, both the Nephites and Lamanites become extremely wicked and continued to divide into further classes according to their riches and pride. Here were created the haves and the have-nots. During this period of iniquity, war broke out and eventually the Nephite nation was totally wiped off the face of the earth.

Has this ever happened before in the history of mankind? Only every time a nation has fallen! Can this happen again? Yes, and it is happening again right now! Today there is no such thing as having all things in common. We definitely have rich and poor, bond and free, "haves," and "have-nots." Classes have once again been established. Pride is raging in the hearts of man. Greed is at an all-time high. We, the inhabitants of this planet, are definitely ripening for destruction.

One might say, "Yes, but the members of the Church are not affected by all this are they?" To this I say, "Look out." We are on the same path the Nephites were on before they fell. All is not well in Zion.

> For behold, ye do love money, and your substance, and your fine apparel, and the adorning of your churches, more than ye love the poor and the needy, the sick and the afflicted. (Mormon 8:37)

Yes, in the Church as with the rest of the world, we find classes, the haves and have-nots. Greed, pride, and speculation are running rampant.

> Why do ye not think that greater is the value of an endless happiness than that misery which never dies—because of the praise of the world?
>
> Why do ye adorn yourselves with that which hath no life, and yet suffer the hungry, and the needy, and the naked, and the sick and the afflicted to pass by you, and notice them not?
>
> Yea, why do ye build up your secret abominations to get gain and cause that widows should mourn before the Lord, and also orphans to mourn before the Lord. (Mormon 8:38–40).

To obtain the praise of the world, members are falling into Satan's favorite traps. Namely the traps of "pride, greed, and class distinction." These crucial traps of Satan eventually lead to other pollutions of the mind and body, the traps that lead to eternal destruction and damnation.

I am afraid that far too many members of the Church are putting their trust in the arm of flesh—in the "gods of silver, and gold, of brass, iron, wood, and stone, which see not, nor hear, nor know" (Daniel 5:23). These are the material things of this earth, the things made by the hand of man. These are idols; they are false gods. "For where your treasure is, there will your heart be also" (Luke 12:34). What we put our heart and trust in becomes our god. If this is something other than the true and living God, then it is idolatry.

Like the people in 4 Nephi, we have been blessed beyond our wildest imaginations with all the good things of the earth. But are we starting to worship them? Are they becoming our false gods? Do they have power over us? Do we have more of these goods than our faith can stand? Are we becoming prideful? Are we becoming greedy? Are we developing classes? The things of the earth—the dead things—have become the idols, the gods of many members.

I know we would like to believe that we are the chosen people and the scriptures are talking about everyone else, but forget that misconception. It is now, and it is us. Just look at all those "Trophy Mansions" that members have sought after and obtained in the last twenty years. Many members living in these prize homes regard themselves as the "upper class" members—a cut above the rest. And the sad thing is that most of the youth of the Church today are striving to be part of that class. After all, that is what is being taught in universities, colleges, and by the precepts of man. In many cases, homes and other material possessions have become our idols and our gods. "But it is not given that one man should possess that which is above another, wherefore the world lieth in sin" (D&C 49:20). "Nevertheless, in your temporal things you shall be equal, and this not grudgingly, otherwise the abundance of the manifestations of the Spirit shall be withheld" (D&C 70:14).

Look at the numerous pyramid marketing schemes that have been created by members in the last few years. Many members are putting their trust in these man-made idols because they are told that if they get involved, they can get rich. It's sad to think about how often we have all been approached "at church" by these people trying to get us involved in their combinations, buying or selling their false gods. Following is what the Lord has to say to them.

> O ye wicked and perverse and stiffnecked people, why have ye built up churches unto yourselves to get gain? Why have ye transfigured the holy word of God, that ye might bring damnation upon your souls? Behold, look ye unto the revelations of God; for behold, the time cometh at that day when all these things must be fulfilled. (Mormon 8:33)

> Love not the world, neither the things that are in the world. If any man love the world, the love of the Father is not in him.
>
> For all that is in the world, the lust of the flesh, and the lust of the

eyes, and the pride of life, is not of the Father, but is of the world.

And the world passeth away, and the lust thereof: but he that doeth the will of God abideth for ever.

Little children, it is the last time: and as ye have heard that antichrist shall come, even now are there many antichrists; whereby we know that it is the last time. (1 John 2:15–18)

The Lord has shown us the way, but we have not fully implemented the Lord's plan as of yet.

And it is my purpose to provide for my saints, for all things are mine.

But it must needs be done in mine own way; and behold this is the way that I, the Lord, have decreed to provide for my saints, that the poor shall be exalted, in that the rich are made low.

For the earth is full, and there is enough and to spare; yea, I prepared all things, and have given unto the children of men to be agents unto themselves.

Therefore, if any man shall take of the abundance which I have made, and impart not his portion, according to the law of my gospel, unto the poor and the needy, he shall, with the wicked, lift up his eyes in hell, being in torment. (D&C 104:15–18)

For a permanent and everlasting establishment and order unto my church, to advance the cause, which ye have espoused, to the salvation of man, and to the glory of your Father who is in heaven;

That you may be equal in the bonds of heavenly things, yea, and earthly things also, for the obtaining of heavenly things.

For if ye are not equal in earthly things ye cannot be equal in obtaining heavenly things;

For if you will that I give unto you a place in the celestial world, you must prepare yourselves by doing the things which I have commanded you and required of you. (D&C 78:4–7)

The Lord has given us the scriptures and modern-day prophets because he knows we need a wake-up call. He knows many of us have the Nephite disease. This disease caused the downfall of the Nephite nation, as well as every other nation that has ever fallen.

The Nephite disease has infected the Saints of today. Many unsuspecting members regard themselves as holy and righteous because they go to church, pay their tithing, and so on. Yet, they have segregated themselves into classes and their hearts are set—at least 6 days of the week—on the gods and idols of this world.

Following is a description of the Nephite disease. This leads to class distinction and eventually to class warfare.

> And it came to pass in the eighth year of the reign of the judges, that the people of the church began to wax proud, because of their exceeding riches, and their fine silks, and their fine-twined linen, and because of their many flocks and herds, and their gold and their silver, and all manner of precious things, which they had obtained by their industry; and in all these things were they lifted up in the pride of their eyes, for they began to wear very costly apparel.
>
> Now this was the cause of much affliction to Alma, yea, and to many of the people whom Alma had consecrated to be teachers, and priests, and elders over the church; yea, many of them were sorely grieved for the wickedness which they saw had begun to be among their people.
>
> For they saw and beheld with great sorrow that the people of the church began to be lifted up in the pride of their eyes, and to set their hearts upon riches and upon the vain things of the world, that they began to be scornful, one towards another, and they began to persecute those that did not believe according to their own will and pleasure.
>
> And thus, in this eighth year of the reign of the judges, there began to be great contentions among the people of the church; yea, there were envyings, and strife, and malice, and persecutions, and pride, even to exceed the pride of those who did not belong to the church of God.
>
> And thus ended the eighth year of the reign of the judges; and the wickedness of the church was a great stumbling block to those who did not belong to the church; and thus the church began to fail in its progress.
>
> And it came to pass in the commencement of the ninth year, Alma saw the wickedness of the church, and he saw also that the example of the church began to lead those who were unbelievers on from one piece of iniquity to another, thus bringing on the destruction of the people.
>
> Yea, he saw great inequality among the people, some lifting themselves up with their pride, despising others, turning their backs upon the needy and the naked and those who were hungry, and those who were athirst, and those who were sick and afflicted. (Alma 4:6–12)

Causes of Class Warfare

Bruce R. McConkie had the following to say about the causes of class warfare.

> Because of iniquity and greed in the hearts of men, there will be depressions, famines, and a frantic search for temporal security–a security sought without turning to the Lord or obeying his precepts. We may expect to see the insatiable desire to get something for nothing result in further class legislation and more socialistic experiments by governments. Economic inequalities will certainly give rise to further class warfare and bickering. There will be riots, bloodshed, hunger, commotion, turmoil, and panics. These are all signs of the times.[1]

In 1832 Joseph Smith received a revelation on war, in which the Lord said that beginning with the rebellion of South Carolina, war would be poured out and would roll forth until it had "made a full end of all nations" (D&C 87). These wars started in South Carolina and since that time there have been all kinds of wars and rumors of wars all over the earth. Many of these wars have been the result of classes rising against each other.

Paul described the apostasy and perilous times of the last days. He described the pride and disregard for anyone but self that leads to the formation of classes and eventually class warfare:

> This know also, that in the last days perilous times shall come.
>
> For men shall be lovers of their own selves, covetous, boasters, proud, blasphemers, disobedient to parents, unthankful, unholy, . . .
>
> Trucebreakers, false accusers, incontinent, fierce, despisers of those that are good,
>
> Traitors, heady, highminded, lovers of pleasures more than lovers of God. (2 Timothy 3:1–4)

Modern revelation describes the wicked conditions that will lead to class warfare as follows:

> Darkness covereth the earth, and gross darkness the minds of the people, and all flesh has become corrupt before my face. Behold, vengeance cometh speedily upon the inhabitants of the earth, a day of wrath, a day of burning, a day of desolation, of weeping, of mourning, and of lamentation; and as a whirlwind it shall come upon all the face of the earth, saith the Lord. (D&C 112:23–24)

The citizens of this country are becoming more and more aware of the gap that is widening between the haves and the have-nots. This greed is what will eventually bring on class warfare in this country and between nations around the world. Following are some examples.

1. American workers pay in the year 2000 was lower, inflation-adjusted, than in 1980 while CEO pay was ten times higher. Workers averaged $28,900 in 1980 and only $28,597–inflation adjusted in 2000. Now compare this with the average CEO of a major corporation who made 1.3 million in 1980 and now makes $13.1 million dollars a year or about $36,000 a day. In 1974 the average CEO made thirty-four times as much as a worker. In 2000 the figure had risen to 485 times as much.[2]
2. It is an undeniable fact that the few have been prospering at the expense of the many in America over the past couple of decades. Our nation has the most unequal distribution of wealth of any industrialized country in the world, with the top one percent owning over 40 percent of America's total wealth. The appalling contempt the super rich have for the classes below them is amazing. Robert T. Holhut writes: "To the contented class, the wealthy are hard-working people blessed by God that are deserving of their good fortune. The poor are lazy, shiftless, and dependent upon handouts and contribute nothing to society. Money given to the wealthy creates jobs. Money provided to the poor saps their moral fiber."[3] It is this kind of thinking that will cause class warfare.
3. In 1970, Dad was working forty hours a week, Mom was just getting into the labor force, and Junior sailed through college on scholarships, selecting any major he liked. As soon as Junior landed his first career job, he got married, bought a house, and raised 2.4 kids. Today, Dad puts in more hours and doesn't dare demand more compensation due to rumors of downsizing. Mom has been working full-time for years, while Junior flipped hamburgers and washed poodles throughout high school. College is essential for anyone who wants a future, so Junior graduated after borrowing

> $20,000 in student loans. He still can't find a decent job because he has no skills. Rents are high, and home prices are worse. He moves back in with Mom and Dad—the so-called boomerang effect. Family health care now requires monthly contributions toward the company's reduced-coverage plan. Social Security will be bankrupt long before Junior is finished paying into it, dad's pension fund was raided during the 1980s. Taxes are higher, the family credit cards are maxed out, and they have no savings. Their old cars are unreliable and repairs are expensive, but the sticker shock on a new one is worse.[4]

The Haves and the Have-nots

When I discuss class warfare, many do not readily grasp the concept, as they are from a background and era that have never thought much about what is happening outside the immediate region where they live. Here I would like to define what class warfare is all about and why it is a great threat to this nation and the entire world.

People generally understand class struggle to be something between the capitalist (ruling or owning) class and the proletariat (or working) class. I think it can be described more completely as the "haves" versus the "have-nots."

When the poor people of the world rise up in these last days, it will be because they will obtained sufficient numbers to be a significant social force. They will believe it is powerful enough to achieve their goal of raising their class to a higher form of life. The class wars that will come about will cover this nation and will engulf the whole earth. They will occur because of the lust for something better, but that better life will not come, because the wars will not provide it for them.

> From whence come wars and fightings among you? come they not hence, even of your lusts that war in your members?
>
> Ye lust, and have not: ye kill, and desire to have, and cannot obtain: ye fight and war; yet ye have not, because ye ask not.
>
> Ye ask, and receive not, because ye ask amiss, that ye may consume it upon your lusts. (James 4:1–3).

The class wars will do one thing, though. The wicked will be fighting against the wicked and they will in due course destroy themselves, the wicked of the earth, and ultimately abolish the classes. They will bring Armageddon as the climax, just prior to the Second Coming of Jesus Christ.

Only when nations have followed God have the people truly been happy and had all things in common, without classes. Throughout the rest of history, because of pride and greed, man has basically divided into three main classes. These include the haves, the have-nots, and those who "have some but want more."

The haves are those with money, power, security, food, luxury, and an abundance of pride and greed. They suffocate in excess with no concern for others, while the have-nots starve. The haves have always been fewest in number, and they want to keep things that way.

The have-nots are by far the greatest in number and growing worldwide. They are grouped together in the misery of poverty, inadequate housing, disease, hunger, despair, and ignorance, with no visible way to get out of this situation. When employment is obtained, they only get jobs that no one else will take, and they are the lowest-paying jobs with few, if any, benefits.

Everyone else falls into the last group, the "have some but want more." In America we call this the middle class. This class is rapidly diminishing as the "haves" want more and leave less for everyone else.

Race is not the discriminating factor in class formation. Classes are formed in economic discrimination, not in the color of one's skin. Each race has its own oppressors that pit one race, group, or class against another.

Conditions Worsen Worldwide

In a recent US Intelligence Report, we learned that hopes for economic globalization bringing on material well-being have been frustrated as gaps between the haves and have-nots have grown wider and will continue to do so for the next fifteen years. The report said that most of Africa, and much of the Middle East, Eastern Europe, South, Central and Southeast Asia, and South America could be left far behind the wealthier and more technologically advanced countries, led by the United States. Regions, countries, and groups left behind will face deepening economic stagnation, and political, ethnic, ideological, and religious extremism, along with the violence that accompanies it. Much of the violence could be directed against the United States. The pre-eminence of the United

States will undoubtedly attract opposition from discontented groups and individuals, who could use anticipated advances in information, communications, and weapons technology to mount terrorist attacks, or information warfare against US territory and interests.[5]

Later, I discuss global population trends and show how the world population is growing by 80 million each year and how the planet is made up of two demographic worlds. One set is the poor, young, and growing countries like Uganda, Nigeria, and all the Moslem countries. The other world is made up of the wealthy, old, and shrinking, which includes most of Europe.[6]

These third world countries that do not have enough food or water to feed and care for their people now, will double and triple in size over the next twenty-five years. We can be assured that as they grow numerically, these have-not nations will look more and more at the have nations and eventually class warfare between nations will erupt.

In the United States, the American economy is producing less and less jobs that pay enough to keep a family out of poverty. The working poor are people who are employed and earn wages, but still live below the poverty line. Some are employed full time, and others can only find part-time work. In both cases, because of low wages, their income level is below the poverty guidelines. In addition, few of these people receive benefits that provide for such things as health care. The number of Americans in this category is growing each year. Of the people in this category, 62.4% of them do have jobs but still cannot make enough to get above the poverty lines.

In the United States if a family earns below the following figures they are living below the poverty line:

Size of Family	**Annual Dollars Earned**
1	$10,400
2	14,000
3	17,600
4	21,200
5	24,800
6	28,400
7	32,000
8	35,600[7]

Source: Federal Register, vol. 73, 15 Jan. 23, 2008, 3971.[7]

More families are being forced to live below the poverty line. "The number of persons below the official government poverty level was 39.3 million in 1993; this was 6.9 million more than 1989."[8] Today the number is still rising and this cannot help but create more problems associated with the haves and the have-nots that will ultimately lead to classes rising against classes, or class warfare within the United States. This will happen just as soon as their numbers become large enough that the poor decide they have had enough of poverty. Then they will band together and mobilize with the intent of taking by force what the rich have.

What Can We Do?

Brigham Young told us what the Prophet Joseph Smith declared: "The time will come when the destiny of the nation will hang upon a single thread. At that critical juncture, this people will step forth and save it from the threatened destruction."[9]

I believe it is our destiny as members of The Church of Jesus Christ of Latter-day Saints to support and defend the Constitution of the United States. I also believe the day will come when the Constitution will hang as by a thread. We will then be called to come forth at that time to be a balance of power, to preserve our Constitution. It will be the responsibility of the elders of Israel who are spread over this nation to rally the righteous of our country and provide the necessary strength to save the institutions of constitutional government.

We must be worthy and willing to follow the Lord and His Prophets at that time. We must also be ready to stand up and fight for what we know is right and of the Lord. President Brigham Young said,

> We all believe that the Lord will fight our battles; but how? Will he do it while we are unconcerned and make no effort whatever for our own safety when an enemy is upon us? . . . it would be quite as reasonable to expect remission of sins without baptism, as to expect the Lord to fight our battles without our taking every precaution to be prepared to defend ourselves. The Lord requires us to be quite as willing to fight our own battles as to have him fight them for us. If we are not ready for an enemy when he comes upon us, we have not lived up to the requirements of him who guides the ship of Zion, or who dictates the affairs of his Kingdom."[10]

We are to stand for right and justice at all times, but it is not for us to decide to take the side of the rich or the poor, as this is choosing one against the other. This is a choice that divides and will expose the image of the beast. Rather ours is to stand in holy places and be on the Lord's side and love our neighbor and show charity to all of God's children.

I believe the Lord has so abundantly blessed us as a people so we can use the resources we have been blessed with to bless all of His other children throughout the world. It is our calling, duty, and responsibility to lead by example.

Now is the time to do all we can to build up the kingdom of God here on the earth. Because the time is rapidly coming that the Lord will once again return to reign as King of Kings and Lord of Lords. No power on earth or in hell can stop this work or frustrate the purposes of the Lord. His word will go forth until it is preached to every nation, kindred, and tongue. The purposes and will of God will be achieved. His children will hear the gospel. This commission to take the Gospel to every nation, kindred, and tongue and people is one of the signs by which we can recognize how close the Savior's coming is at hand. Christ has promised us that this Gospel will go to all the earth. "And this gospel of the kingdom shall be preached in all the world for a witness unto all nations; and then shall the end come" (Matthew 24:14).

Notes

1. Bruce R. McConkie, *Mormon Doctrine,* 2nd ed. (Salt Lake City: Bookcraft, 1966), 728.

2. Paul Krugman, "Haves and Have-Nots—America's Rich Get Richer," (New York Times columnist) Seattle P-1, Jan. 13, 2001.

3. Randolph T. Holhut, "More Thoughts on Republican Class Warfare," at Joyrand@sover.net, 1995.

4. Daniel Brandt, "Class Warfare: Wall Street vs. Main Street," *NameBase Newsline,* no. 13, April-June 1996.

5. Jim Lobe, "Wider Gaps Between Haves and Have-Nots by year 2015," US Intelligence Report. Associated Press, December 18, 2000.

6. Browne Anthony, "Population: The boom heard round the world." *Washington Post.* March 2000.

7. Ohio State University Extension Fact Sheet, "Poverty Fact Sheet Series—The Working Poor," Family and Consumer Sciences, HYG-5703, 98.

8. Lynn H. Ehrie, "Class Warfare /Corporate Welfare: The Vanishing Middle Class," www.Consciouschoice.com, Sep. 1996.

9. Brigham Young, *Journal of Discourses,* 26 Vols. [London: Latter-day Saints Book Depot, 1854-86] 7: 15.

10. Brigham Young, *Discourse of Brigham Young,* selected and arranged by John A. Widtsoe (Salt Lake City: Deseret Book, 1954), 303.

9

FAMINE

> Behold I speak for mine elect's sake; for nation shall rise against nation, and kingdom against kingdom; *there shall be famines*, and pestilences, and earthquakes, in divers places. (Joseph Smith—Matthew 1:29; emphasis added)

Why can we expect these terrible things to come upon the world?

> And again, because iniquity shall abound, the love of men shall wax cold; but he that shall not be overcome, the same shall be saved. (Joseph Smith—Matthew 1:30)

As members of the Lord's Church, what should we do? To begin with, let us do our part to further the work of the Lord:

> And again this Gospel of the Kingdom shall be preached in all the world, for a witness unto all nations, and then shall the end come, or the destruction of the wicked. (Joseph Smith—Matthew 1:31)

Famines will come. In many parts of the earth, they are already here, and it is only going to get worse. We are so blessed as a people, because we have been warned and re-warned by ancient and modern prophets of this time period. If we live by their counsel, we shall be blessed. And we will be able to bless many others at the same time. As members of the Lord's Church, this is how we should look at these times. Because these very hard times will lead to the greatest event we can imagine: The return of Jesus Christ, to reign as King of Kings and Lord of Lords.

Global Population Trends

> For the earth is full, and there is enough and to spare; yea, I prepared all things, and have given unto the children of men to be agents unto themselves. (D&C 104: 17)

I want to begin this section by saying that I truly believe there is enough food on the earth for all of God's children, if we strictly keep the commandments of the Lord.

> And inasmuch as ye do these things with thanksgiving, with cheerful hearts and countenances, not with much laughter, for this is sin, but with a glad heart and a cheerful countenance—
>
> Verily I say, that inasmuch as ye do this, the fulness of the earth is yours, the beasts of the field and the fowls of the air, and that which climbeth upon the trees and walketh upon the earth;
>
> Yea, and the herb, and the good things which come of the earth, whether for food or for raiment, or for houses, or for barns, or for orchards, or for gardens, or for vineyards;
>
> Yea, all things which come of the earth, in the season thereof, are made for the benefit and the use of man, both to please the eye and to gladden the heart;
>
> Yea, for food and for raiment, for taste and for smell, to strengthen the body and to enliven the soul.
>
> And it pleaseth God that he hath given all these things unto man; for unto this end were they made to be used, with judgment, not to excess, neither by extortion. (D&C 59:15–20)

I have been involved in agriculture and agribusiness most of my life. This includes owning a number of farms and agribusinesses, teaching high school agriculture, followed by teaching at the college level, and then serving years as dean of agriculture. Finally, I worked for our government, living in many countries helping farmers, companies, and government leaders improve agriculture and agribusiness in their countries.

From this background and experience in agriculture, I have come to the conclusion that there *is* enough food on this earth to feed all the people who now reside on the earth and all that God will yet send. True, there are famines in numerous countries throughout the earth, and there are millions of hungry people, and many who are dying of starvation. And certainly, most famines are brought about because of natural disasters, such as changes in the weather, water depletion, and soil loss; unfortunately, these conditions are further perpetrated by crime and greed. The problem is not total quantity of food; the world does produce enough food to feed everyone who is now in the world, and it can provide for all those who the Lord will yet send. The problem is *pride* and *greed.* (See chapter 4.)

We can see that the Lord has created all things for the use of man to be used with judgment, not in excess, neither by extortion, but using wisdom in all things. If we do so, there will be enough for all.

With this in mind, let us take a closer look at what is happening today as far as famines are concerned and determine what we as members can and must do. Famines are upon the earth now and will continue to increase in intensity. At this moment, 800 million of the world's population are chronically hungry.[1]

Each of us need to be aware of the fact that the environmental and social impact of population growth knows no national boundaries and affects all of us. Population growth anywhere in the world ultimately has an influence on the entire planet. Environmental problems such as air and water pollution and global climate change have no borders. As the population grows, demands for all resources increase. This ultimately causes an increase in pollution and waste. More energy is needed. The additional energy then increases global warming, acid rain, oil spills, nuclear waste, and so on. More land is required to grow more food, leading to deforestation and soil erosion. More homes, schools, factories, and highways are needed, and this reduces farmland yet further.

Presently, the world population is approximately 6 billion. We add an additional 80 million each year. In 1900, the global population was only 1.6 billion. In the past 100 years we have gained 4.5 billion people. The following table shows our growth rate.

1800	1 billion	All human history
1930	2 billion	130 years
1960	3 billion	30 years
1974	4 billion	14 years
1987	5 billion	13 years
1999	6 billion	12 years

As we began the twenty-first century with 6 billion people, we find there are two demographic worlds. One is poor, young, and growing.

In countries like Uganda and Niger the median age is only fifteen and the population is growing so fast that the population will double in only twenty-three years. In 1950, Nigeria had only 33 million people. By 1995, the population had tripled to 112 million. It is estimated that the population of Niger will triple again by the year 2050 and reach 339 million. And it is very possible it will grow even faster.

The other demographic world is wealthy, old, and shrinking. This includes Europe and other wealthy parts of the world. The median age in Italy and Japan for example is forty. And the population growth in these countries has fallen to zero or below.

Between 1950 and 1995, Europe's share of the world population shrank from 21.7 percent to 12.8 percent. During this same period, Africa's share of the world population increased from 8.9 percent to 12.7 percent. Today, both Europe and Africa each have about one eighth of the world population. This will continue to change drastically in the future. Europe's share of the global population will shrink to about 6.8 percent by 2050 and Africa's share will increase to 21.8 percent. In other words, in one century the population will completely reverse Europe and Africa's position.[2]

From this it would appear that Europe is a demographic catastrophe. If this trend were to continue, Europe and Japan would be ghost towns by the beginning of the next century. We know the Lord has other plans, but if things did continue as they are, that is what would happen.

In a report on population, the Food and Agricultural Organization of the United Nations (FAO) projected that by 2050, one quarter of the developed world will be older than 65. That is a higher proportion of retirement-age people than in Arizona or Florida.[3]

It is quite obvious that the wealthy parts of the world are not producing enough people to sustain themselves. Therefore, the decline of rich nations will most likely change the balance of global political power. We see people from all over the world moving to Europe to take the jobs left by the aging and dying population of Europeans.

How did we get to this point? Maybe it's a change in cultural attitudes. We have gone from a society that believed children were a blessing from God and family duties were a sacred trust, to a society that emphasizes prosperity, greed, and self-indulgence. Most people today believe that families—especially large families—take too much of their time and are too much of a hassle. People of these wealthy countries will soon see that their ancestors were right: Children are a blessing from God, to themselves and to their nations.

Water

Without water there can be no life. Many people in the United States and Europe are not aware of the very critical conditions that now exist on this planet because of both water shortage and the global problems associated with water pollution. Many of the rivers, lakes, streams, oceans and underground aquifers are so polluted that they now poison soil, crops, animals, and humans. I feel it is necessary to bring the following facts out into the open, so we can know how to get ready for the problems of both water shortage and water pollution, as this will be a major cause of famine within a very few years.

An adequate and dependable supply of fresh water is critical for human and animal health, food production, and economic development. Even though two thirds of this planet is covered with water, only a small portion of it about 0.5 to 1.0 percent is available to and usable by mankind.

Presently there are thirty-one countries with about 8 percent of the world's population that have chronic fresh water shortages. Most of these are developing countries that are also experiencing large population growth like Nigeria, Ethiopia, India, and Kenya. By the year 2025, 48 countries are expected to have water shortages that will affect more than 2.8 billion people. This is one third of the world's population.[4]

Much of the world already has polluted water through improper waste disposal. This is stressing the environment and putting more people in life-threatening situations. This condition will only add to the potential for national and international water conflicts leading to additional wars in coming years. Water scarcity is presently the greatest hazard to human health, the environment, and global food supply. Therefore, it threatens world peace as countries in the Middle East and Asia face an ever-decreasing quantity and quality of water.

The people who suffer the most are those living in the world's poorest nations. The major problem caused by water shortage is scarcity of food. If these nations are to survive, they must increase efficiency of irrigation. But this will only help to some extent, as there is still not enough water no matter how efficient they become. In fact, many of the Middle Eastern countries and North African countries have been rapidly depleting their groundwater reserves to the extent that they cannot now, or soon will not be able to, produce enough food to feed the people of their nations.

Salinization and other forms of pollution are occurring in many areas of the Middle East and Asia as well. This is particularly a problem in Pakistan where salt levels are increasing yearly, making it progressively more difficult to grow crops. Raw sewage is polluting the water in many nations to the extent that it is no longer fit for human or animal consumption. Presently, more than a billion people lack safe, clean water and the problem will continue to get worse over the next twenty-five years. A recent United Nations Report found that up to half of the population of the developing world suffers from diseases that come from polluted water.[5]

In many critically water-scarce regions, such as the Arabian Peninsula, North Africa, Northern China, Northwest India, and the Great Plains of the United States, water from deep aquifers is applied to crops faster than it is replaced by rainfall. As this water is depleted the cropland is abandoned, or it reverts to less productive uses.[6]

Another growing problem is that more and more of the earth's available water needed for crops is being appropriated by cities, including Tucson, Los Angles, and Beijing, forcing more and more irrigated cropland out of use. Irrigated land, just 16 percent of total cropland, supplies 40 percent of the grain; therefore each acre of irrigated land lost is of particular concern.[7]

While the developing nations of the world suffer for lack of water, the wealthy nations demand fresh water for industrial development, urbanization, and rising living standards. These demands have increased water usage over 21 percent.[8]

In many parts of the world, the rivers and lakes have become dumping grounds for all kinds of wastes, including untreated sewage, toxic industrial chemicals, and agricultural petrochemical and animal waste runoff. All of the 14 major rivers of India are terribly polluted. Most of China's rivers are unable to support fish and more than 90 percent of the rivers in Europe have high concentrations of nitrates from agrochemicals.[9]

Industrial and municipal pollution presents great threats in developing countries, as 90 to 95 percent of all domestic sewage and 75 percent of all industrial waste is dumped into surface waters without any treatment. But even in Europe and North America, many rivers and lakes have become extremely contaminated with industrial and agricultural pollutants. Throughout the world, we are finding more and more areas where polluted water is causing serious diseases, including malaria, cholera, and typhoid.[10]

The Centers of the Consultative Group on International Agriculture Research published in March 1999 the countries that will be hardest hit with water scarcity in the next twenty-five years. They are listed in order of severity. Category 1 being the worst off presently down to category 4 which will have scarcity to the point they will be in serious trouble within the next twenty-five years.

1. Absolute water scarcity now:
   Afghanistan, Egypt, Iran, Iraq, Israel, Jordan, Kuwait, Libya, Oman, Pakistan, Saudi Arabia, Singapore, South Africa, Syria, Tunisia.

2. Economic water scarcity, now, and getting worse:
   Angola, Benin, Botswana, Burkina Faso, Burundi, Cameroon, Chad, Congo, Cote d'Ivoire, Ethiopia, Gabon, Ghana, Guinea-Bissau, Haiti, Lesotho.

3. Water scarcity now and worsening:
   Albania, Algeria, Australia, Belize, Bolivia, Brazil, Cambodia, Central African Republic, Chile, Colombia, El Salvador, Gambia, Guatemala, Guinea, Honduras, Indonesia.

4. Some water scarcity now and expected to get much worse:
   Argentina, Austria, Bangladesh, Belgium, Bulgaria, Canada, China, Costa Rica, Cuba, Denmark, Dominican Republic, Ecuador, Finland, France, Germany, Greece.[11]

It looks like the prophecies of John about the rivers, lakes, and oceans are beginning to happen:

> And the second angel sounded, and as it were a great mountain burning with fire was cast into the sea: and the third part of the sea became blood;
>
> And the third part of the creatures which were in the sea, and had life, died; and the third part of the ships were destroyed.
>
> And the third angel sounded, and there fell a great star from heaven, burning as it were a lamp, and it fell upon the third part of the rivers, and upon the fountains of waters;
>
> And the name of the star is called Wormwood: and the third part

of the waters became wormwood; and many men died of the waters, because they were made bitter. (Revelations 8:8–11)

SOIL

Almost everything we eat comes from the soil. Next to water, soil is a major cause of famine. Only 11 percent of the earth has arable land, and that land is rapidly diminishing due to erosion, salinization, urban expansion, soil pollution, and poor land management practices.[12]

By 1990, poor land management practices throughout the world had led to the degradation of 562 million hectares or 38 percent of the 1.5 billion hectares of cropland worldwide. Since 1990, soil losses have been 5 to 6 million hectares each year.[13]

The primary cause of agricultural land degradation is soil erosion. Water erosion is responsible for about 66 percent of erosion losses. Wind erosion causes the remaining 34 percent. Topsoil is presently being lost at rates of 16 to 300 times faster than it can be replaced. But it takes between 200 to 1000 years to form one inch of topsoil.[14]

Agricultural land is ruined in other ways as well. Mechanical tilling causes soil compaction and crusting. This ruins soil structure and greatly reduces crop production. Continuous cropping without fallowing, replacing nutrients, or using cover crops, manure, or commercial fertilizer will deplete soil nutrients very rapidly. The over-application of petrochemical herbicides and pesticides and other agricultural chemicals kill beneficial soil organisms.

Poor water management of irrigated land is another major cause of degraded cropland. Poor drainage leads to water logging or salinization of the soil. Salinization is the buildup of salt levels in the soil. This causes the soil to become toxic to both plants and animals. Ten to fifteen percent of all the irrigated cropland in the world is presently affected with either water logging or salinization. These two problems alone represent a great threat to the world's food producing capacity.[15]

Soil losses between 1945 and 1990 alone have reduced world food production capabilities by 17 percent. Regional studies have localized these losses. In Africa, production losses from soil erosion are estimated at just over 8 percent. Data from several different studies indicate that the decline in productivity resulting from soil degradation may exceed 20 percent in a number of Asian and Middle Eastern countries. These losses will continue to get worse as soil degradation continues.[16]

Many hope that genetic engineering of plants will be the answer to world famine, but the facts are that genetic engineering could make the problem even worse. Genetic engineering will lead to more monoculture of plant varieties. In a quest for higher yields, farmers have resorted to fewer and fewer select plant varieties. In ancient times there were hundreds of vegetable varieties, but today only 20 species are used in field cultivation. About 95 percent of our food now comes from 30 plants. For example, only two varieties of peas are planted on 96 percent of our acreage; nine varieties of wheat are raised on 50 percent of our wheat farms; and six varieties of corn are grown on 71 percent of our acreage. This uniformity is what makes crops extremely vulnerable to pests and diseases as the 1970 corn blight demonstrated. The disease attacked only one strain of corn yet destroyed over 700 million bushels.

Continuous cropping associated with monoculture and genetically engineered plants leads to more erosion, which requires heavier use of chemical fertilizers and pesticides to maintain yields. This leaves farmers even more vulnerable, because if disease hits that particular crop or prices drop, their loss will be very high. Also, with the same crop year after year, weeds adapt and flourish. In addition, identical growing seasons over wide areas leads to higher possibilities of drought. No, genetic engineering is not the answer.

President Ezra Taft Benson said:

> We must do more to get our people prepared for the difficult days we face in the future. Our major concern should be their spiritual preparation so they will respond with faith and not fear. "If ye are prepared, ye shall not fear" (D&C 38:21). Our next concern should be for their temporal preparation. When the economies of nations fail, when famine and other disasters prevent people from buying food in stores, the Saints must be prepared to handle these emergencies.[17]

President Spencer W. Kimball said,

> Maintain a year's supply. The Lord has urged that his people save for the rainy days, prepare for the difficult times, and put away for emergencies, a year's supply or more of bare necessities so that when comes the flood, the earthquake, the famine, the hurricane, the storms of life, our families can be sustained through the dark days. How many of us have complied with this? We strive with the Lord, finding many excuses: We do not have room for storage. The food spoils. We do not have the funds

> to do it. We do not like these common foods. It is not needed—there will always be someone to help in trouble. The government will come to the rescue. And some intend to obey but procrastinate.[18]

The latest statistics reveal that less than 6 percent of the members of the Church have an adequate emergency program, which includes a year's supply of food. Each of us knows where we fit into this statistic.[19]

Now is the time for all of us to get our houses in order. I truly believe this and am urging all who will hear to listen and act. Only about 7.2 percent of our population is now actively engaged in farming. Farmers are totally dependent on fuel and transportation to obtain feed, fuel, seed, and fertilizer. Manufactures and processors are also dependent on fuel and transportation to bring the farmers produce to them so they can process and package the food products. Finally, local markets and grocery stores are also dependent on fuel and transportation to get the food to them, so they can ultimately sell it to us the consumers. If anything stops this system, famine could occur within weeks. Food stores would be empty within days and we would all be left to live off our year's supply. That is, if we listened to the prophets, followed their counsel, and have a food supply. For those who did not listen and follow the counsel, the magnitude of the tragedy could be catastrophic.

Let's review a few other things that could cause our food supply to shut down. War will do it—especially when it hits home. Plagues can do the trick very fast. Food contamination from biological warfare used to poison farm animals and crops have been shown to be very effective. These are the obvious things, but what about the less obvious? These include the topics I have just discussed, including the lack of water and water pollution, loss of soil and farms, and the loss of those who are feeding this nation and the world.

Food Storage

God gave both man and animals a natural instinct to preserve our excess food for a time of need. But many of this generation have developed a tendency to squander all they have and leave the future to chance, to others, or to destiny. This is contrary to divine law. We have always been warned to provide for our families, and ourselves and to have on hand a year or two of food for emergencies. This is more important now than ever.

When emergencies strike, the time for preparation has passed.

Remember, it was not raining when Noah built the ark. President Benson said: "More than ever before, we need to learn and apply the principles of economic self-reliance. We do not know when a crisis involving sickness or unemployment may affect our own circumstances. We do know that the Lord has decreed global calamities for the future and has warned and forewarned us to be prepared. For this reason the Brethren have repeatedly stressed a 'back to basics' program for temporal and spiritual welfare."[20]

How long has the Lord warned us? Most believe it has been just since 1936, when the Welfare plan was inaugurated. Actually, for more than 100 years, the Lord has warned us through his prophets to store a year or two of food. In the *Discourses of Brigham Young*, President Young declared the following: "Brethren, learn. You have learned a good deal it is true; but learn more; learn to sustain yourselves; lay up grain and flour, and save it against a day of scarcity. Sisters, do not ask your husbands to sell the last bushel of grain you have to buy something for you out of the stores, but aid your husbands in storing it up against a day of want. . . . And always have a year or two's provision on hand."[21]

Then Wilford Woodruff said: "The Lord is not going to disappoint either Babylon or Zion, with regard to famine, pestilence, earthquake or storms, he is not going to disappoint anybody with regard to any of these things, they are at the doors. . . . Lay up your wheat and other provisions against a day of need, for the day will come when they will be wanted, and no mistake about it. We shall want bread, and the Gentiles will want bread, and if we are wise we shall have something to feed them and ourselves when famine comes."[22]

There are numerous books and publications on food storage and how to do it, but I would like to include some very basic facts on what is needed to survive for one year. Here is another reminder to help everyone remember a year's supply of food is needed for every member of our family.

There are four necessities that one should start with: wheat, dried milk, honey, and salt. After that, you can build up a variety of things your family likes and enjoys.

Many people start collecting food without knowing what they need and in what quantities. Following is a list that many people use as a guideline to fill their basic nutritional needs for their family.

Basic Nutritional Needs for One Year

Pounds per Year

	Adult Male	Adult Female	Male 13–19	Female 13–19	Child 10–12	Child 7–9	Child 4–6	Child 1–3
Wheat	300	200	334	200	200	160	100	70
Other Grains	90	75	139	82	86	65	42	34
Legumes	25	21	41	24	25	19	10	10
Dry Milk	55	45	100	100	100	100	100	100
Food Oils	30	24	46	46	28	21	20	20
Honey/ Sugar	30	20	47	47	29	22	20	20
Dried Fruit	20	17	33	33	20	15	13	13
Shelled Nuts	5	4	7	7	4	3	3	3
Canned Meat	15	12	23	23	15	11	5	5
Vegetables	35	29	54	54	34	26	23	17
Extras	12	10	19	19	12	9	8	6
Yeast	2	2	2	2	2	2	1	1
Seeds	10	10	10	10	8	6	4	2
Salt	5	5	5	5	5	5	5	5

Hard red winter wheat should be used, because it is the highest in protein.

Other grains can include oats, corn, barley, millet, buckwheat, rye, or polished rice. Whole rice is more nutritious, but cannot be stored for long periods of time as it becomes rancid.

Legumes include all beans, including soybeans, peas, and most important, lentils. When we lived in Macedonia, we used lentils as a meat replacement and it was very good. Legumes are very high in protein.

A lot of dried milk products are available. Dried skim milk is the most important to obtain first. It is best stored in number 10 cans. Once the can is opened, it must be used within a short period of time.

Vegetable shortening and cooking oils are needed. These store well for long periods. Again, once opened they should be used in a short period of time.

Honey is the best form of sweetener to store, not only for its sweetening effect, but because it also contains vitamins and minerals that are not found in other sweeteners. But it is always good to have some brown sugar, white sugar, and powdered sugar and possibly sugar substitutes as well. Other alternatives exist, such as blackstrap molasses.

Shelled nuts are high in protein, energy, fat, minerals, and vitamins. They again should be stored in vacuum-sealed number 10 cans. Once opened, they should be consumed within a few months.

Canned meats can include turkey, chicken, tuna, or beef. This will be a very welcome addition to your storage when it is needed.

Vegetables should include home canned vegetables, home dried vegetables, and long storage vegetables dried and/or freeze-dried vegetables in number 10 cans.

The extras to include will depend on the taste buds of your family. My family loves peanut butter, so it is included. Other items may be such things as Jell-O, powdered eggs, dried cheese, powdered whey, cake mixes, noodles and spaghetti, pancake mix, bouillon cubes, onion flakes, dry soup mix, sesame seeds, spices, or whatever else your family likes to eat.

Yeast should be packed and stored in nitrogen. Again, once opened it must be used fairly quickly.

There are two types of seeds: seeds for planting and seeds for sprouting. Garden seeds should include everything you and your family like to eat out of a garden. Get more than you think you will need. Sprouting seeds can include Alfalfa, clover, lentils, and beans. Sprouting is good as it can provide the necessary vitamins, especially vitamin C, which you may not be able to get anywhere else.

The salt you store should be iodized salt. A little iodized rock salt may come in handy too.

In addition to the regular food items, there should be enough multiple vitamins for each member of the family for one year.

Water Storage

Next to air, water is the most important requirement for life, so it is imperative that we have enough water for survival. In addition, most of our food storage is useless unless we have a supply of water to go with it. Therefore, water storage becomes the most important component of our emergency survival plan. We usually need at least four times as much water as food. The average adult needs at least a half gallon of water a day for drinking purposes alone.

But because of the large quantities of water we use, it is often not possible to store a year's supply of water. In addition water stored for long periods of time may become unfit for drinking. So what can we do?

For most families, the easiest and most practical way to store water is in 55-gallon polyethylene water drums. For long-term storage, they must be FDA approved for storing drinking water. Two drums per family member are recommended. Water is relatively inexpensive to store, but the time to do it is now.

Everyone should have as a minimum a two-week supply of emergency water. The amount usually recommended is fourteen gallons per person for a two-week period. Seven gallons per person for drinking and food preparation and another seven gallons per person for other limited uses. Fourteen gallons is enough for subsistence only, which are just two quarts for drinking and two quarts for other purposes per day. If you have room to store more, you probably should do so.

For long-term storage, water should have a disinfectant added. Unscented chlorine based bleach often is used with excellent results. There are also water disinfection tablets available that are made specifically for this purpose.

Non-Food Items

After you have your year's supply of food and an adequate supply of water then the following things should be next on your list.

- First Aid Kit—You can purchase first aid kits that are already stocked with most of the things listed below or you can purchase them separately to fit special needs of your family.

Items that should be considered to be included in a first aid kit, in quantities needed for your family are as follows:

AMA First Aid Guide
½ inch x 10 yards First Aid Tape
Antibacterial deodorant soap
Tweezers
Scissors
Clinical thermometer
Exam quality vinyl gloves
Rubbing alcohol (70 percent)
Hot water bottle
Ice bag
2" x 4.1 yard conforming gauze roll bandages
3" x 4.1 yard conforming gauze roll bandages
4" x 5" instant cold compress
4" x 6" hot /cold reusable compress
6" x ¾" finger splint
6" cotton tipped applicators
3" cotton tipped applicators
¾" x 3" adhesive plastic bandages
3/8" x 1-1/2" junior plastic bandages
2" x 4" elbow & knee plastic bandages
Knuckle fabric bandages
Large fingertip fabric bandages
Large butterfly wound closures
Alcohol cleaning wipes
Soap wipes
Antiseptic cleansing wipes
Antibiotic ointment packs
Burn relief packs
2" x 2" gauze dressing pads
4" x 4" gauze dressing pads
Sterile eye pads

5" x 9" trauma pads
2" x 3" non-stick pads
Decongestant tablets
Ibuprofen tablets
Extra strength non-aspirin tablets
Oil of cloves
Baking soda
Petroleum jelly
Mineral oil
Boric acid
Kaopectate
Baby oil
Calamine lotion
Cornstarch
Epson salts
Hand lotion
Sanitary napkins
Talcum powder
Toilet tissue
Other first aid items, as needed by your family.

Additional items you might include in a storage program might include: Flashlights, battery powered radio, batteries, electrical generator, laundry soap, candles, matches, tooth paste, shaving supplies, warm clothing, bedding, a hand grain grinder, rope, and other items your family uses.

Conquering Fear

Calamities will occur, but if we listen to the Lord and his prophets and do all we can do to prepare, live the commandments and stand in holy places, we will have no need to fear.

> I tell you these things because of your prayers; wherefore, treasure up wisdom in your bosoms, lest the wickedness of men reveal these things unto you by their wickedness, in a manner which shall speak in your ears with a voice louder than that which shall shake the earth; but if ye are prepared ye shall not fear. (D&C 38:30)

Elder John A. Widtsoe spoke in conference during World War II, using D&C 38:30 as his theme. His words were important then and are even more important now than they were in 1942:

> The key to the conquest of fear has been given through the Prophet Joseph Smith. 'If ye are prepared ye shall not fear' (D&C 38:30). That divine message needs repeating today in every stake and ward. Are we prepared to surrender to God's commandments? In victory over our appetites? In obedience to righteous law? If we can honestly answer yes, we can bid fear depart. And the degree of fear in our hearts may well be measured by our preparation by righteous living, such as should characterize Latter-day Saints.[23]

The key to overcoming fear is to live the commandments and follow our prophets. Now is the time to get our food storage in order and then we shall not fear.

> Wherefore, be of good cheer, and do not fear, for I the Lord am with you, and will stand by you; and ye shall bear record of me, even Jesus Christ, that I am the Son of the living God, that I was, that I am, and that I am to come. (D&C 68:6)

> Nevertheless, Zion shall escape if she observe to do all things whatsoever I have commanded her. (D&C 97:25)

Notes

1. FAO Reports and Publications "FAO Special Population Report: The Top Ten List," Washington D.C., October 2001.

2. Browne Anthony "Population The Boom Heard Round the World," *Washington Post,* March 2000.

3. Ibid.

4. Population Reports, "Solutions for a Water-Short World," Population Information Program, Center for Communication Programs, John Hopkins School of Public Health. Baltimore, Maryland. Vol. 14,1998.

5. David Seckler, Randolph Barker and Amarasinghe Upali. Consultative Group on International Agricultural Research (CGIAR) "Water Scarcity in the Twenty-First Century," *International Journal of Water Resources Development.* Washington D.C., March 17, 1999.

6. Ibid.

7. Gary Gardner, Worldwatch paper 131, "Shrinking Fields: Cropland losses

in a World of Eight Billion," July 1996.

8. Danielle Knight, Environment Bulletin, "Water: Worldwide Water Shortage to Worsen," Washington, 1998

9. Ibid.

10. Ibid.

11. David Seckler, Randolph Barker, and Amarasinghe Upali. "Water Scarcity in the Twenty-First Century." *International Journal of Water Resources Development.*

12. C. F. Bentley, Professor Emeritus of Soil Science, "The Production of Good Soil for Food," University of Alberta, Edmonton, 1996.

13. World Resources Institute, "Disappearing Land: Soil Degradation", Washington D.C., gregm@wri.org.

14. Ibid.

15. FAO Reports and Publications, "FAO Special Population Report: The Top Ten List," Washington D.C., Oct. 2001.

16. World Resources Institute, "Disappearing Land: Soil Degradation," Washington D.C., gregm@wri.org

17. Ezra Taft Benson, in Conference Report, Oct. 1980; *Ensign,* Nov. 1980, 32.

18. Spencer W. Kimball, *The Teachings of Spencer W. Kimball,* edited by Edward L. Kimball (Salt Lake City: Bookkcraft, 1982), 374.

19. Food Storage Central, "Helping good people prepare for bad times", Salem, Oregon, director@foodstorage.net.

20. Ezra Taft Benson, in Conference Report, Oct. 1980; *Ensign,* Nov. 1980, 32.

21. Brigham Young, *Discourses of Brigham Young,* 293.

22. Wilford Woodruff, *Journal of Discourses,* vol. 18, 121.

23. John A. Widtsoe, "If Ye Are Prepared," in Conference Report, Apr. 1942, 33–34.

10

Voices, Thunderings, Lightnings, and Earthquakes

> And the angel took the censer, and filled it with fire of the altar, and cast it into the earth: and there were *voices*, and *thunderings*, and *lightnings*, and an *earthquake*. (Revelation 8:5; emphasis added)

Let's discuss each of the four things mentioned, so our understanding will help us to be ready for them. The first was voices. Many people as they read this verse overlook the voices and just think about the thunderings, lightnings, and earthquakes, but in fact the voices are probably the most important part of this verse. The scriptures tell us what is meant by voices.

Voices

> O, ye nations of the earth, how often would I have gathered you together as a hen gathereth her chickens under her wings, but ye would not! How oft have I called upon you by the mouth of my servants, and by the ministering of angels, and by mine own voice, and by the *voice* of thunderings, and by the *voice* of lightnings, and by the *voice* of tempests, and by the *voice* of earthquakes, and great hailstorms, and by the *voice* of famines and pestilences of every kind, and by the great sound of a trump, and by the *voice* of judgment, and by the *voice* of mercy all the day long, and by the *voice* of glory and honor and the riches of eternal life, and would have saved you with an everlasting salvation, but ye would not!" (D&C 43:24–25; emphasis added)

The Lord has tried every way possible to get us to listen, but most have not, because we are too stiffnecked, proud, consumed with the false gods of the world, or afraid of the face of man to put our trust in the Lord. He has tried every way possible to get us to listen. He has given commandments because he loves us and wants us to have all the blessings he has to give in this world and for all eternity. All we have to do is listen and act in accordance to his will. But we will not.

The scriptures portray the events preceding the Second Coming. They describe the voices, which include the voice of the Lord in speech and holy writ, along with his word coming through the elements and forces of nature: the voices of thunderings, lightnings, earthquakes, hailstorms, famines, pestilences, judgment, mercy, glory, and honor (Revelations 8:5, D&C 43:21–25, 88:90, 133:50; Joel 2:11).

In addition, there are the voices of his servants. "And the voice of warning shall be unto all people, by the mouths of my disciples, whom I have chosen in these last days" (D&C 1:4).

"What I the Lord have spoken, I have spoken, and I excuse not myself; and though the heavens and the earth pass away, my words shall not pass away, but shall all be fulfilled, whether by mine own voice or by the voice of my servants, it is the same" (D&C 1:38).

President Ezra Taft Benson discussed the topic of voices in the following quote:

> The voice of warning is unto all people by the mouths of His servants (see D&C 1:4). If this voice is not heeded, the angels of destruction will increasingly go forth, and the chastening hand of Almighty God will be felt upon the nations, as decreed, until a full end thereof will be the result. Wars, devastation, and untold suffering will be your lot except you turn unto the Lord in humble repentance. Destruction even more terrible and far-reaching than attended the last Great War will come with certainty unless rulers and people alike repent and cease their evil and godless ways. God will not be mocked (D&C 63:58). He will not permit the sins of sexual immorality, secret murderous combinations, the killing of the unborn, and disregard for all His holy commandments and the messages of His servants to go unheeded without grievous punishment for such wickedness. The nations of the world cannot endure in sin. The way of escape is clear. The immutable laws of God remain steadfastly in the heavens above. When men and nations refuse to abide by them, the penalty must follow. They will be wasted away. Sin demands punishment.[1]

The Lord is telling us through his prophets what is going to happen if we don't get our act together, listen, and follow the counsel he has given us through his prophets.

> Wherefore, fear and tremble, O ye people, for what I the Lord have decreed in them shall be fulfilled.
>
> And verily I say unto you, that they who go forth, bearing these tidings unto the inhabitants of the earth, to them is power given to seal both on earth and in heaven, the unbelieving and rebellious;
>
> Yea, verily, to seal them up unto the day when the wrath of God shall be poured out upon the wicked without measure. (D&C 1:7–9)

Because man has rejected the gospel and seeks the things of the earth, war, famine, pestilences, and earthquakes will be poured out on the nations of the world.

> And thus, with the sword and by bloodshed the inhabitants of the earth shall mourn; and with famine, and plague, and earthquake, and the thunder of heaven, and the fierce and vivid lightning also, shall the inhabitants of the earth be made to feel the wrath, and indignation, and chastening hand of an Almighty God, until the consumption decreed hath made a full end of all nations. (D&C 87:6)

From the voice of the Lord in the scriptures and the warning voices of past and present prophets, we know that wickedness will continue to increase. We will see an increase in every conceivable form of evil. As man continues to reject the Lord, there will be greater and greater deteriorations of all moral standards and disregard of the Ten Commandments and all commandments of the Lord. The Savior said, "And the love of men shall wax cold, and iniquity shall abound" (D&C 45:27).

I am very thankful that we have prophets of the Lord to lead and guide us by their voices, giving us counsel from the Lord that is needed at this particular time. I am also very thankful that they are not afraid of the face of man and tell it as the Lord would have it said.

An excellent example of the voice of a prophet telling us what we need to hear at this time is the words of President Benson in the following quote:

> We must defend our youth, in the interests of this nation which God has blessed above all others. We must rise to this task, stand up and be counted on the side of decency. We must show by our lives and actions that we possess the virtues that made America great. There

> will be those who will cry "censorship" and "suppressing of freedom of information." To these people there does not seem to be any difference between liberty and license–but there is a real difference. It is not a denial of liberty to forbid the sale of narcotics or alcohol to children, and neither is it a denial of liberty to ban the distribution of filthy, obscene, character-destroying materials. There has developed in this country, I am sorry to say, a species of so-called "broadmindedness" which tolerates anything and everything. It is high time right–thinking citizens showed they are fed up with such false broadmindedness. I for one fail to see where this so-called "tolerance" of evil has made society any better or individuals any happier. We cannot steer a safe course without a compass. We cannot build an enduring society except on principles of righteousness.[2]

The Lord is fully aware of the evils that are consuming the people of this earth today. He loves us and wants to save us and give us all that he has to give, if we will but listen. This is why we have the voices of prophets leading and guiding us today. Each of us has our agency, to choose whom we will follow. As members of the Church, it is very evident that now is the time to follow our prophets today as well as the ancient prophets like Joshua, Alma, and Enoch, when each of them said the same thing: "Choose you this day whom ye will serve; but as for me and my house, we will serve the Lord" (Joshua 24:15; see also Alma 30:8 and Moses 6:33).

Earthquakes

> For after your testimony cometh the testimony of earthquakes, that shall cause groanings in the midst of her, and men shall fall upon the ground and shall not be able to stand. (D&C 88:89)

> For nation shall rise against nation, and kingdom against kingdom: and there shall be earthquakes in divers places, and there shall be famines and troubles: these are the beginnings of sorrows. (Mark 13:8)

> And there shall be earthquakes also in divers places, and many desolations; yet men will harden their hearts against me, and they will take up the sword, one against another, and they will kill one another. (D&C 45:33)

From these verses we can see that after the voices of warnings from the Lord and his prophets, there will be voices of warning of earthquakes.

This will come when the pride of mankind becomes so gross that the sword of vengeance must fall. It appears that we are now living in the time and conditions that was so aptly described throughout the scriptures.

How common are earthquakes? There may be as many as a million quakes each year, if we include those too small to be felt. Earthquakes are common and natural occurring events. The frequency of occurrence of earthquakes based on observations since 1900 is as follows:

Description	Magnitude	Average Annually
Great	8 or higher	1
Major	7–7.9	18
Strong	6–6.9	120
Moderate	5–5.9	800
Light	4–4.9	6,200 (estimated)
Minor	3–3.9	49,000 (estimated)
Very minor	2–3	About 1,000 per day
	1–2	About 8,000 per day[3]

How much energy is released in each earthquake? Earthquakes are extremely destructive because of the great energy released. The following table shows the magnitude of the earthquake and the approximate tons of TNT needed to release the same amount of energy.

Magnitude	Approximate TNT Energy
4.0	6 tons
5.0	199 tons
6.0	6,270 tons
7.0	199,000 tons
8.0	6,270,000 tons
9.0	99,000,000 tons[4]

The scriptures discuss the last days when there will be earthquakes in diverse places. "For nation shall rise against nation, and kingdom against kingdom: and there shall be famines, and pestilences, and earthquakes, in diverse places" (Matthew 24:7).

Following is a list of earthquakes that caused deaths in 2001 alone. Look at the magnitude and diverse places of these earthquakes.

Date	Magnitude	Place	Deaths
13 Jan 2001	7.7	El Salvador	852
26 Jan 2001	7.7	India	20,023
13 Feb 2001	6.6	El Salvador	315
17 Feb 2001	4.1	El Salvador	1
23 Feb 2001	5.6	Sichuan, China	3
24 Mar 2001	6.8	Western Honshu Japan	2
19 Apr 2001	5.6	Yunnan, China	2
08 May 2001	5.4	El Salvador	1
23 May 2001	5.3	Sichuan, China	2
01 Jun 2001	5.0	Afghanistan	4
21 Jun 2001	4.2	Germany	1
23 Jun 2001	8.4	Coast of Peru	139
07 Jul 2001	7.6	Coast of Peru	1
17 Jul 2001	4.7	Northern Italy	4
24 Jul 2001	6.3	Northern Chile	1
09 Aug 2001	5.5	Central Peru	4
27 Oct 2001	5.7	Yunnan, China	1
04 Dec 2001	5.8	Southern Peru	2
Total			21,358[5]

The largest earthquake to be recorded with modern equipment since 1900 occurred on 22 May 1960 in Chile. This earthquake measured 9.5 on the Richter scale. In this earthquake more than two thousand people died, three thousand more were injured, and nearly two million lost their homes. This earthquake caused an estimated $550 million in damage, and the destruction didn't end there. This particular earthquake also caused an additional 61 deaths and $75 million damages in Hawaii, 138 deaths and $50 million damages in Japan, 32 deaths in the Philippines, and $500,000 in damages to the west coast of the United States.[6]

The 1960 earthquake was indeed a very large and terrible one, but we know from the scriptures, it is nothing in comparison to the "great" earthquake that will occur just prior to Christ's Second Coming, as foretold in Revelation.

> And there were voices, and thunders, and lightnings; and there was a great earthquake, such as was not since men were upon the earth, so mighty an earthquake, and so great. (Revelation 16:18)

Then in the next two verses John tells just how great this earthquake will be:

> And the great city was divided into three parts, and the cities of the nations fell: and great Babylon came in remembrance before God, to give unto her the cup of the wine of the fierceness of his wrath. And every island fled, away, and the mountains were not found. (Revelation 16:19–20)

Why do you think the Lord will need to put on such a demonstration? Could it be because he has tried everything else and it has not worked? Could it be that mankind has become so evil that the Lord has no other choices? What will the majority of the earth's population be like when this happens? The following passages in Mormon show what mankind will be like when these things happen. What is our world like right now? How long do you think the Lord can tolerate this constant acceleration of evil and darkness that is presently consuming the earth?

What Will the World Be Like When These Things Come?

In the eighth chapter of Mormon, the time and conditions are described in a way that looks far too familiar with the world we are presently living in:

And it shall come in a day when the blood of saints shall cry unto the Lord, because of secret combinations and the works of darkness.

Yea, it shall come in a day when the power of God shall be denied, and churches become defiled and be lifted up in the pride of their hearts; yea, even in a day when leaders of churches and teachers shall rise in the pride of their hearts, even to the envying of them who belong to their churches.

Yea, it shall come in a day when there shall be heard of fires, and tempests, and vapors of smoke in foreign lands;

And there shall also be heard of wars, rumors of wars, and earthquakes in divers places.

Yea, it shall come in a day when there shall be great pollutions upon the face of the earth; there shall be murders, and robbing, and lying, and deceivings, and whoredoms, and all manner of abominations; when there shall be many who will say, Do this, or do that, and it mattereth not, for the Lord will uphold such at the last day. But wo unto such, for they are in the gall of bitterness and in the bonds of iniquity.

Yea, it shall come in a day when there shall be churches built up that shall say: Come unto me, and for your money you shall be forgiven of your sins.

O ye wicked and perverse and stiffnecked people, why have ye built up churches unto yourselves to get gain? Why have ye transfigured the holy word of God, that ye might bring damnation upon your souls? Behold, look ye unto the revelations of God; for behold, the time cometh at that day when all these things must be fulfilled.

Behold, the Lord hath shown unto me great and marvelous things concerning that, which must shortly come, at that day when these things shall come forth among you.

Behold, I speak unto you as if ye were present, and yet ye are not. But behold, Jesus Christ hath shown you unto me, and I know your doing.

And I know that ye do walk in the pride of your hearts; and there are none save a few only who do not lift themselves up in the pride of their hearts, unto the wearing of very fine apparel, unto envying, and strifes, and malice, and persecutions, and all manner of iniquities; and your churches, yea, even every one, have become polluted because of the pride of your hearts.

For behold, ye do love money, and your substance, and your fine apparel, and the adorning of your churches, more than ye love the poor and the needy, the sick and the afflicted.

O ye pollutions, ye hypocrites, ye teachers, who sell yourselves for that which will canker, why have ye polluted the holy church of God? Why are ye ashamed to take upon you the name of Christ? Why do ye not think that greater is the value of an endless happiness than that misery which never dies—because of the praise of the world?

Why do ye adorn yourselves with that which hath no life, and yet suffer the hungry, and the needy, and the naked, and the sick and the afflicted to pass by you, and notice them not?

Yea, why do ye build up your secret abominations to get gain, and cause that widows should mourn before the Lord, and also orphans to mourn before the Lord, and also the blood of their fathers and their husbands to cry unto the Lord from the ground, for vengeance upon your heads?

Behold, the sword of vengeance hangeth over you; and the time soon cometh that he avengeth the blood of the saints upon you, for he will not suffer their cries any longer. (Mormon 8:27–41)

From this and all other evidence before our eyes, it would appear that the "great" earthquake is nigh at hand, as well as all the other obliteration that is prophesied to happen. And it would be well to remember, "All these are the beginning of sorrows" (Matthew 24:8).

Thunderings and Lightnings

All the prophets have warned us that before the Second Coming of the Lord there will be many signs by which the righteous may know that the day of the Lord is near. The Savior told us that before his coming wars and rumors of wars should be heard, the whole earth would be in commotion, and men's hearts should fail them. The Lord told us through his prophet Joseph Smith that after the testimony of the servants of God in these days wrath and judgments will come upon the people; there will be a testimony of earthquakes that will cause groanings in the midst of the earth; there will be the testimony of thunderings, of lightnings, of tempests, the waves of the sea heaving themselves beyond their bounds, and all things will be in commotion.

George Q. Cannon observed,

An age of disasters is the present. All the signs foretold by the Savior and the Prophets which were to precede the Second Coming of the Lord are being witnessed at the present time. The news that comes to us every day over the wires brings word of calamities of every description. We hear of cyclones, of shipwrecks, of floods, of the sea heaving itself beyond its bounds, of earthquakes, of collisions upon railroads, of murders and suicides, of wars and rumors of wars, until the ear is vexed with the tidings. We read of more calamities in one day than formerly were known in a month. Yet, these things have come along so gradually that men attach no importance to them. Though they are intended as signs of the coming of the Lord and the near approach of the end, mankind fail to perceive in these events any of the signs which the Prophets have described.[7]

The Lord has warned us,

> For after your testimony cometh the testimony of earthquakes, that shall cause groanings in the midst of her, and men shall fall upon the ground and shall not be able to stand. And also cometh the testimony of the voice of thunderings, and the voice of lightnings, and the voice of tempests, and the voice of the waves of the sea heaving themselves beyond their bounds. (D&C 88:89–90)

Many today are like the people of Noah's day who did not believe there would be a flood. They continued in their evil ways, even after the warnings of Noah. The floods came, the people were destroyed, and the earth was cleansed of their presence.

The Lord has thoroughly warned the people of today of the judgments we can expect if we do not repent. Destruction will come upon us as a whirlwind. The Lord also warned us what would happen if the people hardened their hearts against the testimony of his servants:

> For a desolating scourge shall go forth among the inhabitants of the earth, and shall continue to be poured out from time to time, if they repent not, until the earth is empty, and the inhabitants thereof are consumed away and utterly destroyed by the brightness of my coming. Behold, I tell you these things, even as I also told the people of the destruction of Jerusalem; and my word shall be verified at this time as it hath hitherto been verified. (D&C 5:19–20)

> But, behold, in the last days, or in the days of the Gentiles—yea, behold all the nations of the Gentiles and also the Jews, both those who shall come upon this land and those who shall be upon other lands, yea, even upon all the lands of the earth, behold, they will be drunken with iniquity and all manner of abominations—And when that day

shall come they shall be visited of the Lord of Hosts, with thunder and with earthquake, and with a great noise, and with storm, and with tempest, and with the flame of devouring fire. (2 Nephi 27:1–2)

Notes

1. Ezra Taft Benson, *The Teachings of Ezra Taft Benson* (Salt Lake City: Bookcraft, 1992), 73–74.

2. Ibid., 412.

3. M. Zirbes, USGA National Earthquake Information Center. Updated 2 January 2002.

4. The University of Memphis, Center for Earthquake Research and Information. Updated 18 September 2001.

5. M. Zirbes, USGA National Earthquake Information Center. Updated 02, January 2002.

6. Institute of Geological and Nuclear Sciences of New Zealand.

7. George Q. Cannon, *Gospel Truth: Discourses and Writings of President George Q. Cannon*, 24:452.

11

Go Ye into All the World

And he said unto them, Go ye into all the world, and preach the gospel to every creature. He that believeth and is baptized shall be saved; but he that believeth not shall be damned. (Mark 16:15–16)

And verily I say unto you, the rest of my servants, go ye forth as your circumstances shall permit, in your several callings, unto the great and notable cities and villages, reproving the world in righteousness of all their unrighteous and ungodly deeds, setting forth clearly and understandingly the desolation of abomination in the last days.

For, with you saith the Lord Almighty, I will rend their kingdoms; I will not only shake the earth, but the starry heavens shall tremble.

For I, the Lord, have put forth my hand to exert the powers of heaven; ye cannot see it now, yet a little while and ye shall see it, and and that I will come and reign with my people.

I am Alpha and Omega, the beginning and the end. (D&C 84:117–20)

How soon will the Second Coming be? The Savior provides some general answers in Matthew 24. He describes the great calamities that will precede his Second Coming and then gives the parable of the fig tree:

Now learn a parable of the fig tree; When his branch is yet tender, and putteth forth leaves, ye know that summer is nigh; So likewise ye, when ye shall see all these things, know that it is near, even at the door. Verily I say unto you, this generation shall not pass, till all these things be fulfilled. Heaven and earth shall pass away, but my words shall not pass away. (Matthew 24:32–35)

From this we can tell that the time is near, yes very near, but in the very next verse he let us all know that no one knows the exact time. "But of that day and hour knoweth no man, no not the angels of heaven, but my Father only" (Matthew 24:36).

So the question cannot be answered by pointing to a date on a calendar. Rather, a chain of events have been prophesied that must occur before Christ returns.

Many of these things have already happened, and many more are taking place now, such as the gathering of the Jews to Israel, the wars and rumors of wars, and the plagues that are starting. Two of the most important events that have to happen before the Second Coming are the restoration of the gospel in the last dispensation and the Book of Mormon being made available to the world as a second witness of Jesus Christ. These things have happened. Now the next important event can happen and, indeed, has already begun. The restored gospel must be taught to every nation, kindred, tongue, and people. And after this has happened the end will come.

"And again, this Gospel of the Kingdom shall be preached in all the world, for a witness unto all nations, and then shall the end come, or the destruction of the wicked" (Joseph Smith—Matthew 1:31). We know that the restored gospel will be preached to the entire world in the last days:

> And I saw another angel fly in the midst of heaven, having the everlasting gospel to preach unto them that dwell on the earth, and to every nation, and kindred, and tongue, and people, Saying with a loud voice, Fear God, and give glory to him; for the hour of his judgment is come: and worship him that made heaven, and earth, and the sea, and the fountains of waters. (Revelation 14:6–7)

In modern times we have been told now is the time to take the restored gospel to the entire world:

> Go ye into all the world, preach the gospel to every creature, acting in the authority which I have given you, baptizing in the name of the Father, and of the Son, and of the Holy Ghost. And he that believeth and is baptized shall be saved, and he that believeth not shall be damned. (D&C 68:8–9)

And in fulfillment of what we read in Revelation, we read further in Doctrine and Covenants:

> And now, verily saith the Lord, that these things might be known among you, O inhabitants of the earth, I have sent forth mine angel flying through the midst of heaven, having the everlasting gospel, who hath appeared unto some and hath committed it unto man, who shall appear unto many that dwell on the earth.
>
> And this gospel shall be preached unto every nation, and kindred, and tongue, and people.
>
> And the servants of God shall go forth, saying with a loud voice: Fear and God and give glory to him, for the hour of his judgment is come. (D&C 133:36–38)

On March 8, 1833, Joseph Smith received a revelation in Kirtland, Ohio that started the work:

> For it shall come to pass in that day, that every man shall hear the fulness of the gospel in his own tongue, and in his own language, through those who are ordained unto this power, by the administration of the Comforter, shed forth upon them for the revelation of Jesus Christ. (D&C 90:11)

In the Book of Mormon, we learn that all will have the opportunity to hear the gospel in their own tongue:

> For behold, the Lord doth grant unto all nations, of their own nation and tongue, to teach his word, yea, in wisdom, all that he seeth fit that they should have; therefore we see that the Lord doth counsel in wisdom, according to that which is just and true. (Alma 29:8)

In 1970 President Benson made the following statement: "No power on earth or in hell can stop this work or thwart the purposes of the Lord to have His soul-satisfying gospel message go to His children. It may take war, commotion, disasters of many forms to bring it about. But the purposes of God will be achieved. His children will hear the gospel of salvation in His own due time."[1]

The work is now well under way. As of this writing, there are 348 missions with over 53,000 missionaries teaching the gospel in approximately 120 different countries around the world. At the Provo MTC there are now fifty languages taught to missionaries so they can teach people in their own tongue. The book of Mormon has now been translated into seventy five languages. In addition, selections of the Book of Mormon have been translated into thirty other languages. Presently, the restored gospel of Jesus Christ is being taught in all areas of the earth except the Moslem speaking countries, China, parts of Africa, parts of Asia, and Israel. These areas and countries will be opened to the preaching of the gospel when the Lord sees that we are ready to handle the task at hand. There will be churches and eventually temples established in these lands.

Will large numbers of people be brought into the Church? In comparison to the number of people on the earth, the number of Church members will be very small because of wickedness, but there will be wonderful faithful members all over the world with congregations in every country.

> And it came to pass that I beheld the church of the Lamb of God, and its numbers were few, because of the wickedness and abominations of the whore who sat upon many waters; nevertheless, I beheld that the church of the Lamb, who were the saints of God, were also upon all the face of the earth; and their dominions upon the face of the earth were small, because of the wickedness of the great whore whom I saw. (1 Nephi 14:12)

Even though the number in comparison to total world population will be low, the actual number will be great.

> After this I beheld, and lo, a great multitude, which no man could number, of all nations, and kindreds, and people, and tongues, stood before the throne, and before the Lamb, clothed with white robes, and palms in their hands; and cried with a loud voice, saying, Salvation to our God which sitteth upon the throne, and unto the Lamb. (Revelation 7:9–10)

Daniel gives us some ideas how many this number is—so many that no man could count:

> A fiery stream issued and came forth from before him: thousand thousands ministered unto him, and ten thousand times ten thousand stood before him: the judgment was set, and the books were opened. (Daniel 7:10)

From this we can deduct that when Christ returns there will be a very large number of devout members. This will be a number far in excess of the number of members we have in the Church today. We can also see the importance of missionary work and the necessity for each of us doing our part in the "every member a missionary" program.

> Behold, I sent you out to testify and warn the people, and it becometh every man who hath been warned to warn his neighbor. (D&C 88:81)

We have a good start on missionary work, but the great days of missionary work are still ahead. We must go to all nations and do far more in the countries we are already in. The everlasting word will go forth as the Lord has decreed.

The gospel is going forth for the purpose of saving souls. The missionaries are the servants of the Lord; they have been called to labor in his fields. They are going forth to reap; and, as it has always been, the harvest is great and the laborers are few. This is why every member has been called to be a missionary.

> Behold, the field is white already to harvest; therefore, whoso desireth to reap, let him thrust in his sickle with his might, and reap while the day lasts, that he may treasure up for his soul everlasting salvation in the kingdom of God. Yea, whosoever will thrust in his sickle and reap, the same is called of God. (D&C 6:3–4)

A wonderful promise has been given to the faithful laborers of the Lord.

> Verily, verily, I say unto you, I who speak even by the voice of my Spirit, even Alpha and Omega, your Lord and your God—
>
> Hearken, O ye who have given your names to go forth to proclaim my gospel, and to prune my vineyard.
>
> Behold, I say unto you that it is my will that you should go forth and not tarry, neither be idle but labor with your might—
>
> Lifting up your voices as with the sound of a trump, proclaiming the truth according to the revelations and commandments which I have given you.
>
> And thus, if ye are faithful ye shall be laden with many sheaves, and crowned with honor, and glory, and immortality, and eternal life. (D&C 75:1–5).

In 1986 President Ezra Taft Benson gave us the secret of missionary work: "The greatest secret of missionary work is work! If a missionary works, he will get the Spirit; if he gets the Spirit, he will teach by the Spirit; and if he teaches by the Spirit, he will touch the hearts of the people and he will be happy. There will be no homesickness, no worrying about families, for all time and talents and interests are centered on the work of the ministry. Work, work, work—there is no satisfactory substitute, especially in missionary work."[2]

How Will the Task Be Accomplished?

The day is rapidly approaching when every corruptible thing will be consumed and there will be a new heaven and a new earth whereon dwelleth righteousness. But until that day, the harvest will go forward under increasingly difficult circumstances, because the world is becoming more and more evil and ripening in iniquity. War, plagues, pestilence, and desolation will cover the earth before the Lord comes; yet the preaching of the gospel will go forward in the midst of all these trials and conflict. And who has the Lord called to accomplish this task? He has called on us—you and me!

> The weak things of the world shall come forth and break down the mighty and strong ones, that man should not counsel his fellow man, neither trust in the arm of flesh—But that every man might speak in the name of God the Lord, even the Savior of the world. (D&C 1:19–20)

Is this exciting or what!

> And if men come unto me I will show unto them their weakness. I give unto men weakness that they may be humble; and my grace is sufficient for all men that humble themselves before me; for if they humble themselves before me, and have faith in me, then will I make weak things become strong unto them. (Ether 12:27)

How does the Lord plan to have the restored gospel preached to all the world? Again, the Lord said he will use us, the weak things of the world, to get the job done:

> Wherefore, I call upon the weak things of the world, those who are unlearned and despised, to thrash the nations by the power of my Spirit;
>
> And their arm shall be my arm, and I will be their shield and their buckler; and I will gird up their loins, and they shall fight manfully for me; and their enemies shall be under their feet; and I will let fall the sword in their behalf, and by the fire of mine indignation will I preserve them.

> And the poor and the meek shall have the gospel preached unto them, and they shall be looking forth for the time of my coming, for it is nigh at hand. (D&C 35:13–15)

It would appear that the statement by the Lord "to let the sword fall in behalf of his servants" must mean that the wars that are happening between the nations of the earth will bring down walls and open these nations for the preaching of the restored gospel of Jesus Christ. In this way, the doors will be opened to the poor and meek, and they will accept the gospel. As the faithful and humble servants of the Lord go quietly about teaching the gospel during all the desolation, they will gather those who are willing to accept Jesus as the Christ and live the commandments of the Lord and become members of his Church.

So what is the best thing we as members can do now and during all the perils that are coming? Yes, there will be many that will turn directly against the Church and its members, and many nations will gather against the Lord's people.

> Now also many nations are gathered against thee, that say, Let her be defiled, and let our eyes look upon Zion. But they know not the thoughts of the Lord, neither understand they his counsel: for he shall gather them as the sheaves into the floor. (Micah 4:11–12)

The best thing we can do when the wicked forces come against us is to preach the gospel to them just as Ammon and his companions did to the Lamanites. By so doing we will set an example and soften their hearts and eventually things will turn around.

> But in the last days it shall come to pass, that the mountain of the house of the Lord shall be established in the top of the mountains, and it shall be exalted above the hills; and people shall flow unto it. And many nations shall come, and say, Come, and let us go up to the mountain of the Lord, and to the house of the God of Jacob; and he will teach us of his ways, and we will walk in his paths: for the law shall go forth of Zion, and the word of the Lord from Jerusalem. (Micah 4:1–2)

Before this time comes there will be great tribulation upon the whole face of the earth:

> And in that generation shall the times of the Gentiles be fulfilled.
> And there shall be men standing in that generation, that shall not

> pass until they shall see an overflowing scourge: for a desolating sickness shall cover the land.
>
> But my disciples shall stand in holy places, and shall not be moved; but among the wicked, men shall lift up their voices and curse God and die. (D&C 45:30–32)

Throughout this entire time we will preach the gospel every day to every creature because we have been commissioned to do so. We in this Church have a solemn obligation to carry the message of salvation to our Father's other children in the world. To us the Lord has given this command: "Go ye into all the world, preach the gospel to every creature" (D&C 68:8).

Every Member a Missionary

The Lord has said, "For behold, this is my work and my glory—to bring to pass the immortality and eternal life of man" (Moses 1:39). Therefore, our major concern should also be the spreading of the gospel to all of God's other children, our brothers and sisters.

Elder Bruce R. McConkie said:

> This call to missionary service does not leave us any choice or option as to the course we should pursue. It is not merely a permissive invitation which allows us to spread the gospel message on a voluntary basis, or if we find it convenient to do so. The decree is mandatory. We have no choice about it, if we are to retain the favor of God. The Lord has laid upon our shoulders the obligation to spread the gospel, to raise the warning voice, to gather in the lost sheep of the house of Israel. If we neglect to do so, we have violated our trust and failed to comply with a divine directive.[3]

This responsibility has been placed on us. The Lord has sent us to this earth under very favorable circumstances and has provided us with many blessings so we can use our time, talents, energy, education, and other resources to bless all of his children by sharing the gospel with them. We cannot be saved unless we help save God's other children. This is a great responsibility, yet one we humbly accept. We have been called to take the gospel to every person on the earth with no exception and no excuse. We cannot judge who is ready to hear the gospel; we are to take it to all of God's children: "Go ye into all the world, and preach the gospel to every creature" (Mormon 9:22).

President Spencer W. Kimball said,

> Do we really believe in revelation? Then why cannot we accept fully as the revealed word of God the revelation of the Prophet-President David O. McKay, wherein he brought to the Church and to the world this valuable Church slogan, "Every Member a Missionary"? How else could the Lord expect to perform His work except through the Saints who have covenanted to serve Him? You and I have made such a covenant. Will we honor our sacred covenant?[4]

If each member of the Church would help bring one other member into the Church each year, it would only take 9.8 years until every person on the earth could be a member. Now, I realize this will not happen, because everyone has his or her agency to choose, but this shows just how fast the gospel can be taught to every person on the earth if each of us did our part in the "Every Member a Missionary" program.

Regarding our responsibilities to teach the gospel, President Benson said,

> This commission to take the gospel to every nation, kindred, tongue, and people is one of the signs by which believers will recognize the nearness of the Savior's return to earth. Concerning this sign of His second coming, Jesus prophesied: "And this gospel of the kingdom shall be preached in all the world for a witness unto all nations; and then shall the end come" (Matthew 24:14). This task will require thousands of missionaries, many more than are presently engaged in worldwide missionary service today. You are needed in the service of the Lord today as never before. The harvest truly is great, but the labourers are few (Luke 10:2).[5]

If we don't share the gospel with others, I think it is because we are either disobedient or wimps. I define "wimps" to be those who are so afraid of the face of man that they will not share with others their most valuable possession, their knowledge of the truthfulness of the gospel of Jesus Christ. We know those who are disobedient sadden the Lord. And likewise, the Lord is not pleased with wimps:

> But with some I am not well pleased, for they will not open their mouths, but they hide the talent which I have given unto them, because of the fear of man. Wo unto such, for mine anger is kindled against them. And it shall come to pass, if they are not more faithful unto me, it shall be taken away, even that which they have. (D&C 60:2–3)

Another thing the Lord does not appreciate is those who are lazy or idle.

> Behold, they have been sent to preach my gospel among the congregations of the wicked; wherefore, I give unto them a commandment, thus: Thou shalt not idle away thy time, neither shalt thou bury thy talents that it may not be known. (D&C 60:13)

> Thou shalt not be idle; for he that is idle shall not eat the bread nor wear the garments of the laborer. (D&C 42:42)

And the Lord is especially concerned with sluggards:

> Go to the ant, thou sluggard; consider her ways, and be wise:
> Which having no guide, overseer, or ruler,
> Provideth her meat in the summer, and gathereth her food in the harvest.
> How long wilt thou sleep, O sluggard? when wilt thou arise out of thy sleep?
> Yet a little sleep, a little slumber, a little folding of the hands to sleep. (Proverbs 6:6–10)

If we are called to preach the gospel to every creature, and we have been called to do so, then the Lord expects excellence and dedication from those He has called. No wimps. No fear of the face of man. No idlers. No sluggards. The Lord needs an army of dedicated saints who He can count on to go into all the world and share the gospel with every creature.

A Time to Prepare

Now is the time to prepare. Now is the time to learn what is in the scriptures. Now is the time to get acquainted with the Lord so we can follow him and teach others to do the same. No man can be saved in ignorance.

> Let him that is ignorant learn wisdom by humbling himself and calling upon the Lord his God, that his eyes may be opened that he may see, and his ears opened that he may hear; For my Spirit is sent forth into the world to enlighten the humble and contrite, and to the condemnation of the ungodly. (D&C 136:32–33)

How can we serve the Lord if we continue to waste our time watching the boob tube? We cannot justify time wasted watching TV. The scriptures say it very clearly:

> How long, ye simple ones, will ye love simplicity? And the scorners delight in their scorning, and fools hate knowledge? Turn you at my reproof: behold, I will pour out my spirit unto you, I will make known my words unto you. (Proverbs 1:22–23)

Now is the time to seek for more than the boob tube and other short-sighted "numbing and dumbing" activities. Now is the time to get to know God and seek the kingdom of God. The scriptures tell us, "But seek ye first the kingdom of God, and his righteousness; and all these things shall be added unto you" (Matthew 6:33).

In other words, now is the time to:

1. Get to know the Lord through prayer and scripture study.
2. Trust in the Lord and strive to do his will.
3. Put our priorities in order; the Lord is first, our neighbor is second, and we are a distant third. We must learn to forget ourselves.
4. Leave the materialistic things of the world behind.
5. Overcome the fear of the face of man.
6. Seek knowledge, understanding, and wisdom.
7. Listen to the Spirit, so we can be taught and guided by the Spirit.
8. Always practice the Golden Rule.
9. Never do anything we would not do if Christ were standing next to us.

Then we will be ready to serve the Lord the way he expects us to. Then we will be in a position to bring many of God's other children to Him. We will then have the ability to teach by example, and teach with the spirit; the only true way to teach. "And the Spirit shall be given unto you by the prayer of faith; and if ye receive not the Spirit ye shall not teach" (D&C 42:14).

I especially appreciate what Elder Boyd K. Packer said about our responsibility to preach the gospel to every individual on the earth: "We accept the responsibility to preach the gospel to every person on the earth. And if the question is asked, 'You mean you are out to convert the entire world? Why, that's impossible! It cannot be done!' To that we simply say, 'Perhaps, but we shall do it anyway.' "[6]

In 1978, Elder Bruce R. McConkie made the following remarks

about missionary work in a speech at BYU. Today we can see that some of it has already happened, and the rest will come to pass in the Lord's time.

> Some day, in the providence of the Lord, we shall get into Red China and Russia and the Middle East, and so on, until eventually the gospel will have been preached everywhere, to all people; and this will occur before the second coming of the Son of Man. . . . I have no hesitancy whatever in saying that before the Lord comes, in all those nations we will have congregations that are stable, secure, devoted, and sound. We will . . . have progressed in spiritual things to the point where they have received all of the blessings of the house of the Lord. That is the destiny. . . . People from all nations will have the blessings of the house of the Lord before the Second Coming.[7]

That statement is particularly close to me as I have had the opportunity of living in many parts of the former Soviet Union and watching the Church grow in those countries. There are now congregations in each of these countries, and in Russia there are presently eight missions. It has been announced that a temple will be built in Ukraine, and I am sure many more will follow, as they are needed in the rest of the former Soviet Union. The gospel will proceed to go forth until it is preached everywhere to all people. I fully expect that one of my sons will have the opportunity to teach the gospel in China in the near future as he already speaks Mandarin Chinese, having served two years in Taiwan on his mission. He has kept up with the language by teaching the Taiwan Air Force how to fly F-16 fighter jets. He has had the opportunity to go to mainland China for our government on several occasions.

President Gordon B. Hinckley said: "The Church needs you. The Lord needs you. The world needs you. There are many out there who need exactly what you have to offer. They are not easy to find, but they will not be found unless there are those who are prepared and willing to seek them out."[8]

This is a wonderful time to be living and have the opportunity to share the gospel with our brothers and sisters around the world. The Lord will sustain us in our missionary efforts if we have the faith to try.

> And thou shalt declare glad tidings, yea, publish it upon the mountains, and upon every high place, and among every people that thou shalt be permitted to see.

> And thou shalt do it with all humility, trusting in me, reviling not against revilers. . . .
>
> And speak freely to all; yea, preach, exhort, declare the truth, even with a loud voice, with a sound of rejoicing, crying—Hosanna, hosanna, blessed be the name of the Lord God!
>
> Pray always, and I will pour out my Spirit upon you, and great shall be your blessing—yea, even more than if you should obtain treasures of earth and corruptibleness to the extent thereof. (D&C 19:29–30, 37–38)

We have truly been called at this time to be a light unto the world. We have been called to be an example and to show our brothers and sisters the way back to the Lord. To be a light unto the world is a wonderful calling, responsibility, and opportunity we have been entrusted with.

> Ye are the light of the world. A city that is set on an hill cannot be hid. Neither do men light a candle, and put it under a bushel, but on a candlestick; and it giveth light unto all that are in the house. Let your light so shine before men, that they may see your good works, and glorify your Father which is in heaven. (Matthew 5:14–16)

If we are humble and dedicated, study, pray for guidance by the Spirit, open our mouths, fear not the face of man, and put our trust in the Lord, then we will become a light unto the world and we will be successful in this most important calling of sharing the gospel with every creature. We will then know how to address every situation and how to talk to every person because we will be guided by the Spirit.

> And it shall be given thee in the very moment what thou shalt speak and write, and they shall hear it, or I will send unto them a cursing instead of a blessing. For thou shalt devote all thy service in Zion; and in this thou shalt have strength. (D&C 24:6–7)

Now the Lord does not say everything will go without any problems. There will be many trials and afflictions, but we are to continue to open our mouths and declare the gospel and we will receive the needed strength to accomplish every task.

> Be patient in afflictions, for thou shalt have many; but endure them, for, lo, I am with thee, even unto the end of thy days. And at all times, and in all places, he shall open his mouth and declare my gospel as with the voice of a trump, both day and night. And I will give unto

> him strength such as is not known among men. (D&C 24:8, 12)

As we follow this counsel and put our trust in the Lord, we will be greatly blessed and will be able to accomplish our missionary responsibilities as the Lord would have us do.

> Therefore, if you will ask of me you shall receive; if you will knock it shall be opened unto you.
>
> Now, as you have asked, behold, I say unto you, keep my commandments, and seek to bring forth and establish the cause of Zion.
>
> Seek not for riches but for wisdom; and, behold, the mysteries of God shall be unfolded unto you, and then shall you be made rich. Behold, he that hath eternal life is rich.
>
> Verily, verily, I say unto you, even as you desire of me so it shall be done unto you; and, and if you desire, you shall be the means of doing much good in this generation.
>
> Say nothing but repentance unto this generation. Keep my commandments, and assist to bring forth my work, according to my commandments, and you shall be blessed. (D&C 11:5–9)

In conclusion, war, famine, pestilences, plagues, earthquakes, and every other form of misery are conditions that we must prepare for. These are judgments to be poured out on all nations because of the rejection of the gospel of Jesus Christ.

> And thus, with the sword and by bloodshed the inhabitants of the earth shall mourn; and with famine, and plague, and earthquake, and the thunder of heaven, and the fierce and vivid lightning also, shall the inhabitants of the earth be made to feel the wrath, and indignation, and chastening hand of an Almighty God, until the consumption decreed hath made a full end of all nations. (D&C 87:6)

We should not be surprised to see wickedness increase. We can expect to see an increase in all moral problems and every other form of evil. The Savior said; "And the love of men shall wax cold, and iniquity shall abound" (D&C 45:27).

Now let's review how the Lord wants us to live, how he intended us to live, how we must live if we are to be the Lord's people.

> And it came to pass in the thirty and sixth year, the people were all converted unto the Lord, upon all the face of the land, both Nephites

> and Lamanites, and there were no contentions and disputations among them, and every man did deal justly one with another.
>
> And they had all things common among them; therefore there were not rich and poor, bond and free, but they were all made free, and partakers of the heavenly gift. . . .
>
> And it came to pass that there was no contention in the land, because of the love of God, which did dwell in the hearts of the people.
>
> And there were no envyings, nor strifes, nor tumults, nor whoredoms, nor lyings, nor murders, nor any manner of lasciviousness; and surely there could not be a happier people among all the people who had been created by the hand of God.
>
> There were no robbers, nor murderers, neither were there Lamanites, nor any manner of -ites; but they were in one, the children of Christ, and heirs to the kingdom of God. (4 Nephi 1:2–3, 15–17)

And what would be the additional benefits of truly being the Lord's people.

> And there were great and marvelous works wrought by the disciples of Jesus, insomuch that they did heal the sick, and raise the dead, and cause the lame to walk, and the blind to receive their sight, and the deaf to hear; and all manner of miracles did they work among the children of men; and in nothing did they work miracles save it were in the name of Jesus. (4 Nephi 1:5)

This is how we must become, if we are going to be a light unto the world, and truly be the Lord's "chosen" people. We must become a people that the Lord can count on, a people who are 100 percent dedicated to serving the Lord and our fellow man. Presently, we have a long way to go, yes a very long way to go. We must start by cleaning the inner vessel of greed, vanity, and pride. We must not only be willing to die for the Lord, but to live for the Lord.

We have been saved to come forward in this the last day to bring souls unto Christ. This is the most important thing we can possibly do. Though desolation, wars, and, plagues will transpire, the only hope for mankind is the gospel of Jesus Christ. We have been called to bring the gospel to all the world, so let's get on with the job!

> And now, behold, I say unto you, that the thing which will be of the most worth unto you will be to declare repentance unto this people,

that you may bring souls unto me, that you may rest with them in the kingdom of my Father. Amen. (D&C 15:6)

The *only* hope for this world is the gospel of Jesus Christ.

Notes

1. Ezra Taft Benson, in Conference Report, Apr. 1970; *Improvement Era,* June 1970, 96.

2. Ezra Taft Benson, "The Secret of Missionary Work," Texas San Antonio Mission, March 2, 1986.

3. Bruce R. McConkie, in Conference Report, Oct. 1960, 54.

4. Spencer W. Kimball, Regional Representatives Seminar, Salt Lake City, Utah, September 30, 1977.

5. Ezra Taft Benson, in Conference Report, Apr. 1984; *Ensign,* May 1984, 43–44.

6. Boyd K. Packer, *Ensign,* Nov. 1975, 97.

7. Bruce R. McConkie, "All are Alike Unto God," Religious Educators Symposium, Salt Lake City, LDS Church Educational System, 1979, 3.

8. Gordon B. Hinckley, "The Question of a Mission," *Ensign*, May 1986, 40.

LET US HEAR THE CONCLUSION OF THE WHOLE MATTER: FEAR GOD, AND KEEP HIS COMMANDMENTS: FOR THIS IS THE WHOLE DUTY OF MAN.

—ECCLESIASTES 12:13

Appendix

Codified Natural Laws

1. You can have anything you want, if you help enough other people get what they want.

Exodus 2:16–22
Proverbs 11:25, 14:21
Matthew 7:21
D&C 1:10

2. Learn the art of delegation, share the load, share responsibilities, and share the rewards.

Exodus 18:13–27
Numbers 11:16–17
Deuteronomy 1:13
D&C 107:99

3. Make time and interest work for you, not against you. Lenders are rulers, borrowers are servants.

Deuteronomy 15:6, 28:12
Matthew 5:42
Proverbs 22:7
D&C 136:25–27
Mosiah 4:28

4. Only through self-discipline and doing what is difficult can people become the individuals they really want to be.

Proverbs 10:4–5, 12:24, 12:27, 22:29
1 Corinthians 9:24–25
D&C 88:124

5. As dogs return to their vomit, the unwise return to bad habits.

Proverbs 26:11 3 Nephi 7:8 2 Peter 2:22

6. Prudent men hold their tongues; fools proclaim foolishness.

Proverbs 11:12–13, Proverbs 12:23, 17:27–28 Proverbs 29:11 Amos 5:13 James 1:19

7. Pride and arrogance precede the fall of both men and nations.

Leviticus 26:19–20 Proverbs 13:10, 16:18 Isaiah 2:12 Matthew 23:12 2 Nephi 28:15 D&C 90:17

8. He who loves sleep and pleasure must endure poverty.

Proverbs 6:6–11, 20:13, 24:30–34
D&C 88:124

9. Choose your friends—don't let them choose you. Walk with the wise; a companion of fools will be destroyed.

Proverbs 9:6, 13:20, 22:24
James 4:4

10. Joy belongs to the man with principles, he who masters self and lives what he knows and believes.

Proverbs 2:10–11, 21:15, 25:28 Isaiah 51:11 Luke 6:23 D&C 51:19 2 Nephi 9:18 Mosiah 2:41

11. Happiness and honor come to those who get ahead of themselves—not those who try to get ahead of others.

Proverbs 27:2 Romans 12:21 Revelation 2:26, 3:21, 21:7 D&C 63:47, 76:53.

12. If you believe, any goal is possible . . . if you work hard enough and smart enough to earn it.

2 Chronicles 20:20 Proverbs 3:5–6 Matthew 8:13 Mark 11:24 D&C 35:8

13. Take a hold of and honor instruction, for happy is the man that obtains knowledge. When knowledge accompanies diligence and discretion, one obtains understanding. Combine humility with understanding, and the prize is wisdom. Wisdom is far more precious than silver or gold; the reward is peace of mind, satisfaction, happiness, length of days, and ultimate riches and honor.

Proverbs 2:2–11, 3:13–21, 4:7, 5:1–2, 8:1–14, 9:6–10
D&C 1:26, 88:118–119

14. A compassionate answer terminates anger and demonstrates understanding. One who holds his tongue is considered wise and regarded as a man of discretion and discernment.

Proverbs 13:3, 15:1
Zechariah 7:9–10
1 Peter 3:8–10
D&C 121:41–45

15. Happiness comes from creation, sorrow from destruction. By our choices, we create or destroy ourselves.

Proverbs 3:13–20
2 Nephi 2:11–30
Alma 3:26–27
4 Nephi 4:15–17
D&C 59:23)

16. What we think about *is* what we are.

Proverbs 16:3, 23:7
Mark 7:20–23
Luke 6:45
Philippians 4:8
Alma 12:14
D&C 18:38, 88:67, 121:45

17. Concentrating on the present and ignoring the future is vanity, which renders eternal vexation.

Ecclesiastes 1:14, 2:11, 2:17, 2:26, 6:9
Isaiah 65:13–15
D&C 87:5–6

18. Man's duty is to reverence God and keep his commandments.

Deuteronomy 4:40, 5:6–21, 6:17
Proverbs 4:4, 7:2
Ecclesiastes 12:13
1 John 2:3–6
1 Nephi 2:10
Mosiah 2:22

Matthew 5:19, 22:37–38	D&C 58:26, 59:21, 93:20
John 14:15	

19. Honesty and integrity build individuals and nations of strength.

Proverbs 12:22, 15:4	2 Corinthians 4:2, 8:21
Luke 8:15;	1 Thessalonians 4:12
Romans 12:17, 13:13	D&C 51:9

20. Freedom is the reward of those who obey the laws of God.

Exodus 19:5	Isaiah 1:19–20
Deuteronomy 4:40	D&C 64:34–36, 98:8–17
Job 36:11–12	Articles of Faith 1:3

21. A virtuous life produces strength of character, peace of mind, and genuine and eternal happiness.

Psalms 24:3–5	2 Peter 1:3–11
Proverbs 12:4, 31:10–31	D&C 4:6, 25:2, 121:45
Philippians 4:8	Articles of Faith 1:13

22. Sin cannot produce happiness. Sin renders misery and vexation.

Leviticus 26:28	Isaiah 59:2	John 8:21, 8:34
Deuteronomy 24:16	Jeremiah 5:25, 40:3	Mormon 7:12
Proverbs 5:22, 14:8–9	Matthew 5:19	D&C 88:86

23. Excellence and quality of workmanship reveal how one feels about himself and his God.

Proverbs 17:27	Philippians 1:9–11
Proverbs 24:3–6	Heb. 11:4
Daniel 6:3	

24. To reach new and higher goals, a man must do that which he never required of himself before.

Job 1:1, 8	2 Corinthians 13:11
Proverbs 4:18	Colossians 3:14
Matthew 5:48, 19:21	D&C 50:24, 67:13
Luke 6:40	

25. What we attain is not as important as what we could have accomplished with greater diligence. Work is the difference between average and genius.

Proverbs 10:4–5, 12:24, 12:27, 22:29
2 Corinthians 8:7
Alma 32:42
Mormon 9:6
D&C 58:26–29, 59:3–4
D&C 75:3, 28–29, 90:24
D&C 103:96, 130:18–19

26. To find happiness, forget yourself and help others

Deuteronomy 22:1–4
Proverbs 14:21–22, 19:17
Matthew 16:24–26
John 13:14–17

27. Lasting happiness comes from giving, not receiving.

Psalms 112:9
Proverbs 21:26, 25:21, 28:27
Matthew 10:8
Mark 10:21
Luke 6:30, 38
2 Corinthians 9:7–11
Mosiah 4:15–24

28. Integrity is the foundation of nobility.

1 Kings 9:4
Job 2:3, 27:1-8, 31:6
Proverbs 11:1-8, 20:7
James 1:5–9
Alma 53:20
D&C 124:15–20

29. In all things, strive for temperance and self-mastery, so you can lead by example with discretion, discernment, and judgment.

Proverbs 23:19–23
Matthew 23:23–33
1 Corinthians 9:25
Galatians 5:22–23
Philippians 4:5
Titus 1:8
2 Peter 1:4–8
Alma 7:23–24, 38:10–12;
D&C 4:6, 12:8, 107:30

30. Strong drink is a liar and thief. It promises happiness and joy but renders only misery and vexation as it robs your wealth, friends, family, health, and finally life.

Leviticus 10:9
Numbers 6:3
Deuteronomy 32:33
Isaiah 28:7–8
Habakkuk 2:15–17
1 Corinthians 3:16–19, 6:9–10

Judges 13:4, 14
Proverbs 20:1, 23:21, 29–32
Ecclesiastes 10:17
Isaiah 5:20–24, 24:9
Galatians 5:21
1 Timothy 3:3
2 Nephi 15:11
D&C 89:5, 7, 136:24

31. The Lord gave us our body and our mind. What we do with them demonstrates what we think of ourselves and how much we love the Lord.

Deuteronomy 5:6–21, 6:4–6
Romans 12:1–2
1 Corinthians 3:16–17, 6:15–20
2 Corinthians 6:13–18
1 Thessalonians 4:3–5
2 Timothy 2:19–22
Mosiah 2:36–37
Alma 40:23–26
Mormon 6:21
D&C 84:33–34, 88:28, 89, 93:35

32. Complete freedom is obtained only when one lives all the laws and commandments of God with exactness.

Proverbs 13:13–18, 29:18
Isaiah 2:2–3, 51:7
Romans 7:21–25
James 2:10, 2:17–26
Ether 8:22–25
D&C 29:34–35, 30:11, 41:5
D&C 42:59, 88:34–35, 98:5–15

33. Tell me who your friends are and I will tell you who you are.

Proverbs 17:17, 18:24, 22:24–25
Proverbs 27:6, 9–10, 17
Luke 14:12–14
James 4:4
Alma 17:2–3
D&C 121:9

34. Never let what you cannot do get in the way of what you can do.

Luke 18:1
Ephesians 6:12–17
Hebrews 12:1–2
Revelation 3:5, 12, 21, 21:7
D&C 63:47–48, 76:53–60

35. One must be true to himself before he can be true to others.

Proverbs 14:25
Zechariah 7:9–10
Luke 16:10–12
Revelation 3:7
Articles of Faith 1:13

36. Share wisdom with a fool and he will despise you. Share wisdom with the prudent and he will honor you.

Psalm 37:30–32
Proverbs 1:7, 9:6–10, 13:1
Proverbs 15:5–12, 23:9, 24:7
Matthew 7:6
D&C 41:6

37. Today's planning determines tomorrow's accomplishments.

2 Corinthians 6:2
2 Nephi 2:21, 27
Alma 12:24, 34:32, 42:4
D&C 1:12, 78:5–7, 109:8

38. Anything and everything is possible to him who believes. If one believes something is impossible he has made it so for himself.

Proverbs 3:5–6, 16:20, 28:25
Matthew 8:13
Mark 9:23, 11:24
John 3:15–18, 14:12–14
Romans 1:16
James 1:5–6
D&C 84:116

39. Beware of those who call evil good and good evil, who say darkness is light and light is darkness, or bitter is sweet and sweet is bitter. These are they who lead those who follow straight to hell.

Isaiah 5:20
2 Nephi 15:20
Mosiah 7:13–19
D&C 121:16–25

40. If you want others to be happy, extend genuine love. If you want to be happy, extend genuine love.

Leviticus 19:18, 19:34
Matthew 5:43–47
Mark 12:30–31
Luke 6:27–30, 35
Luke 10:27
Romans 13:9
Galatians 5:14
James 2:8
Mosiah 23:15
3 Nephi 12:44
D&C 59:6

41. A man can run away from where he is, but not from what he is.

Proverbs 2:2–11, 6:16–19, 20:7
Alma 53:20

42. Thoughts precede acts, acts precede habits, habits precede character, and character precedes our eternal reward.

Proverbs 23:7
Matthew 12:33–37
Galatians 6:7–8
Philippians 4:8–9
Alma 12:14
D&C 101:78

43. Success is not measured in what you have but in what you are.

Proverbs 10:2, 15:16
Ecclesiastes 5:10
Matthew 6:19–21, 12:35
Mark 8:35-38
Luke 12:29–34
Jacob 2:19
D&C 1:16

44. When righteous people are in power, the citizens rejoice, but when the wicked rein the subjects mourn. Choose ye well.

Proverbs 28:28, 29:2
Matthew 15:14, 20:26–28
Mosiah 5, 20:26–28
D&C 98:8–10

45. If you are offered something at no cost, consider it. If it is virtuous, honorable, and uplifting, take two and share with others. If it is vile, repulsive, or downgrading, immediately retreat and never look back.

Philippians 4:8
Alma 5:40–42
Articles of Faith 1:13
Moroni 7:12
D&C 4:5–7

46. The weak cannot forgive, because forgiveness is manifested only in the strong.

Matthew 6:14–16, 18:21–22
Luke 6:37
D&C 64:10, 98:38–48

47. Only those who demonstrate genuine love and are void of pride and vanity can preach without being preachy.

Proverbs 4:18, 8:13
Matthew 5:14–16
Romans 12:12–18
D&C 88:121

48. Gratitude is the beginning of understanding.

Deuteronomy 8:10–11
Malachi 3:8–12
Mosiah 2:20–21
Alma 38:14
D&C 46:7, 46:32,
D&C 59:21, 136:28–32

49. The beginning of understanding is to know the proper order of things: the Lord is first, our neighbor is second, and self is third. Wisdom and happiness are obtained when we live this principle.

Deuteronomy 4:6–9
Proverbs 1:2–7, 2:2–11
Romans 11:33
1 Corinthians 1:20, 25–31
James 1:5–6
Mosiah 2:17
Alma 4

50. Our entire duty is to fear God and keep his commandments.

Ecclesiastes 12:13
John 14:15
Alma 36:1, 30
D&C 25:15, 58:2, 59:5

51. This life is given to us so we can properly prepare for the next one, as that is the real one.

Matthew 19:16–17
Romans 6:23
Revelation 21:7–8
Alma 34:31–35
D&C 6:7
D&C 76:53–70

52. Only by forgetting himself can one find true and lasting joy.

Matthew 16:24–26
Mark 8:34
1 Corinthians 13
Revelation 2:7, 26, 21:7–8
Mosiah 3:19
Alma 38:11–12

53. Those who are afraid of the face of man, seek the praise of man, or pursue the vain things of this world have forsaken God and have chosen a bitter path.

Psalms 56:11
Isaiah 51:12
Jeremiah 1:8
Matthew 6:2
Hebrews 11:23–27
D&C 98:14–17, 121:34–40

54. We must choose hot or cold, light or darkness—there are no gray areas. Excellence is what God requires of us; anything less is mediocrity, which is of the devil.

Psalms 112:4–9
Proverbs 4:18–19
Isaiah 5:20–22
Revelation 3:15–16
Moroni 7:13–19
2 Nephi 15:20–22
D&C 121:16–17

55. Freedom is earned by living the commandments. Those who sin are the servants of sin.

Genesis 4:7;
Deuteronomy 24:16;
Proverbs 5:22;
Proverbs 10:12;
Matthew 5:19;
Romans 3:20;
Hebrews 3:13;
D&C 50:29, 93:1

56. The rewards of living the commandments and using wisdom in all things is ultimate length of life and quality of life.

Job 28:28
Proverbs 1:2–7, 2:6
Proverbs 2:13, 4:7–11
Proverbs 16:16, 24:3–7
Isaiah 33:6
James 1:5
Mosiah 2:17
Alma 37:35
D&C 1:26, 76:5–10

57. You are what you are because that is exactly what you want to be. You can become much more, yes, anything you want to be, if you desire it enough to work for it, have enough faith that it will happen, and then expect it to happen. Then it will happen.

Psalms 90:16–17
Matthew 21:22
Mark 11:24
John 14:12–14;
3 Nephi 18:20
Mormon 9:21
D&C 29:6

58. People become what you expect them to be. Treat everyone *as if* they are champions, and they will become just that. You get what you expect out of everyone including yourself. Expect the most out of others and yourself, and you will get it.

Proverbs 17:27
Daniel 6:3
Matthew 5:14–16
Matthew 5:43–48, 7:12
1 Corinthians 13:1–13
Galatians 5:22
Ephesians 4:29–32
Philippians 2:1–5
Colossians 2:12–15
Hebrews 13:1
James 1
D&C 38:24
D&C 64:33
D&C 121:45–46

59. The entire gospel in one word is obedience.

Exodus 19:5–6
Deuteronomy 5:27, 6:3
Joshua 24:24
Samuel 15:22
Jeremiah 7:23, 11:4
Matthew 7:21–24
Luke 11:28
John 7:17
Romans 5:19
2 Nephi 33:15
Mosiah 2:33
D&C 56:3
D&C 130:20–21
Articles of Faith 1:3

60. We give our lives to that which we give our time.

Proverbs 18:9
Ecclesiastes 3:1–9, 8:5
2 Nephi 9:27
Alma 34:33
D&C 75:3

INDEX

S

T

U

V

W

Y

Z

About the Author

His life has been spent in production agriculture, agribusiness, teaching, international agribusiness, scripture study, and missionary work.

His world of work began with hands-on ownership and management of farms and agribusinesses. He owned two dairy farms, and a sheep ranch and was president and CEO of an International Bull Stud. Next he served as Northwest Program Director for the Holstein Friesian Association. His teaching background began as a high school vocational agriculture teacher. Later he was hired by Oregon State University where he taught Dairy Science and managed the Dairy Research Farm.

Then he went on to Northcentral Technical College in Wausau, Wisconsin, and served as Associate Dean of Agriculture and the Trade and Industry programs. While at Northcentral Technical College, he wrote grants that made it possible to bring more than one hundred students from Former Soviet Union countries to the U.S. for training in Wisconsin. During this time he was able to go to many of these countries and learn much that would help him in later years.

He was then hired as Country Director, with Volunteers in Overseas Cooperative Assistance (VOCA), working in the countries of Macedonia and Ukraine and other parts of the former Soviet Union to help farmers and agribusinesses establish a free market economy after years of communism.

Shortly after he returned to the United States he was called to serve as Mission President of the Russia Samara Mission. This mission is large and covers three time zones. During this three year time period he covered many miles and saw how agriculture was failing and felt the need to write this book, *Opening the Seventh Seal,* to help members understand the signs of the times.

After his mission to Russia, he took twenty-one BYU students to China to teach English. While there he was able to write much of this book.

Soon after this he was called on another mission, to serve as Chair of the Animal Science Department at BYU—Idaho. While there he had the opportunity to study the scriptures more in depth and understand what will happen in the last days.

For the past two years he has served yet another mission at Welfare Square in Salt Lake City. He has been serving as a bishop, helping the homeless and transients. During this period he has been able to see what life will be like for more people in the coming years.

0 26575 52651 6